Notes from the Publisher

Welcome to a glimpse into the world of international [quilting]. [Our hope] is for you to be able to explore beyond the boundari[es of your country] and see what other fiber artists are doing.

In many countries, rather than learning from [many teachers,] under a single master, spending years progressing from simple techniques to the extremely difficult. Intricate designs are celebrated, and sewing and quilting by hand is honored, and as such, hand quilting is the typical method used to quilt.

This book was written in its original language, Japanese, by a master quilter, Yoko Saito. We have done our best to make the directions for each project easy to understand if you have some level of quilting experience, while maintaining the appearance and intent of the original author and publisher.

We hope the beautifully designed handmade items in this book inspire and encourage you to make them for yourself.

- Important Tips Before You Begin -

The following facts might suggest that intermediate or advanced quilters will be more comfortable working on these projects.

- Techniques -

It is rare for Ms. Saito to go into detailed descriptions of specific quilting or sewing methods for each project. She assumes that the creator is familiar with sewing, quilting, and bag-making techniques to some degree and thus relies heavily on the creator's ability to figure out the directions that are not specifically written out. It is advisable to read through and understand each project's direction page from beginning to end, including finding the corresponding patterns before beginning.

- Measurements -

The original designs were created using the metric system for dimensions. In order to assist you, we have included the imperial system measurements in brackets. However, please note that samples that appear in the book were created and tested using the metric system. Thus, you will find that if you use the imperial measurements to make the projects, the items you make will not be exactly the same size as when using the metric measurements.

- Patterns/Templates -

Full pattern information for each project appears in two different ways: a) in the materials list and b) in the illustrations and captions. One must read through all the instructions carefully to understand what size to cut the fabric and related materials, including instructions for each project relating to seam allowances.

- Notions/Accessories -

Some of the projects in this book will call for a variety of accessories such as zippers, handles, and hardware. While the originals were made with items from Japan, most, if not all of the accessories have comparable items or are available around the world. However, some of the accessories are available through Yoko Saito's quilt shop in Japan. See the copyright page for further information.

Stitch Publications, 2021

Yoko Saito's
Handheld Patchwork Treasures

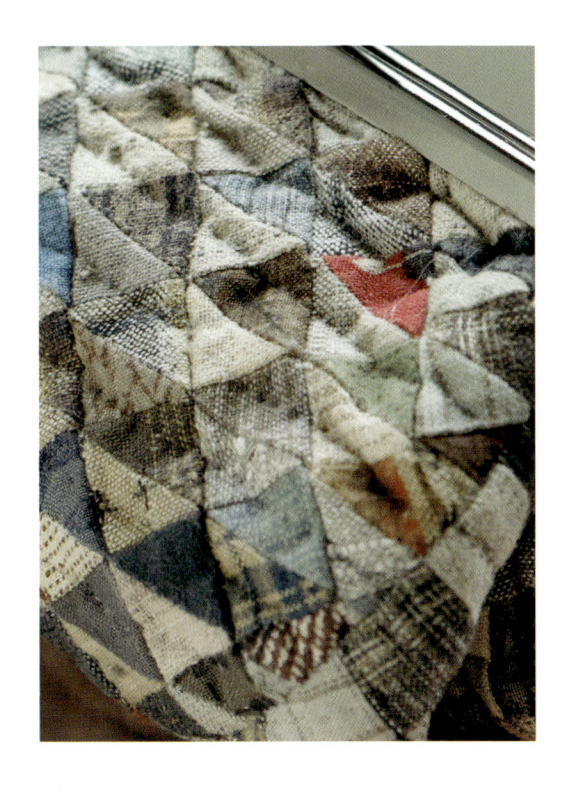

Perfectly Small and Lovely Projects

by Yoko Saito

Introduction

In between the large quilts that I work on, which are so time-consuming, I love to make small and pretty items that work up fairly quickly and fit in the palms of my hands.

Creating such small items means that the seam allowances must be tiny and more attention must be given to the stitches and finishing, but the result is incredibly satisfying.

I hope you not only make one or two for yourself, but that you also make some of these items as gifts for friends or loved ones. Use these items for organization in your handbag or around the house.

May you enjoy these handheld treasures as much as I do.

Yoko Saito

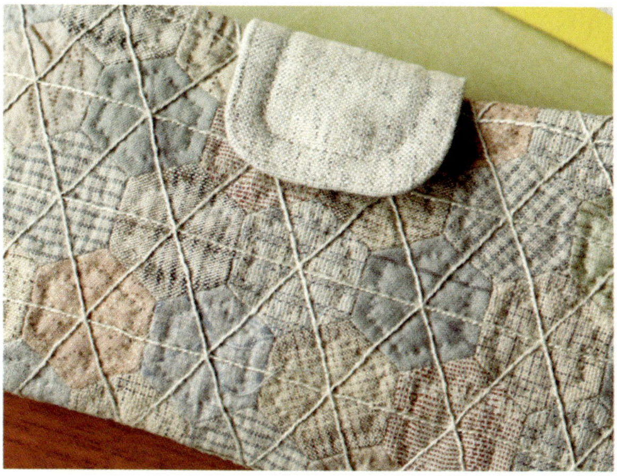

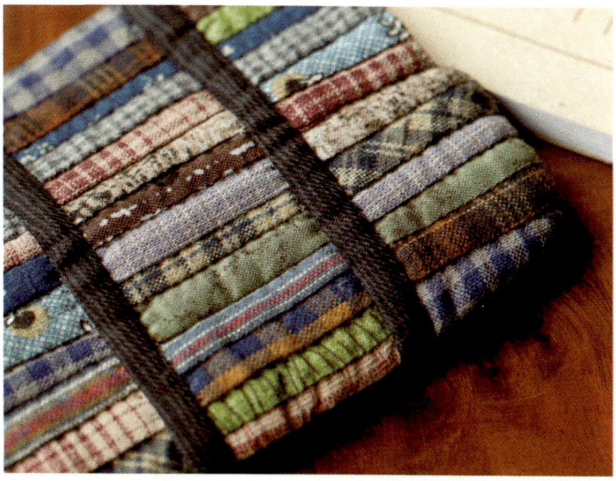

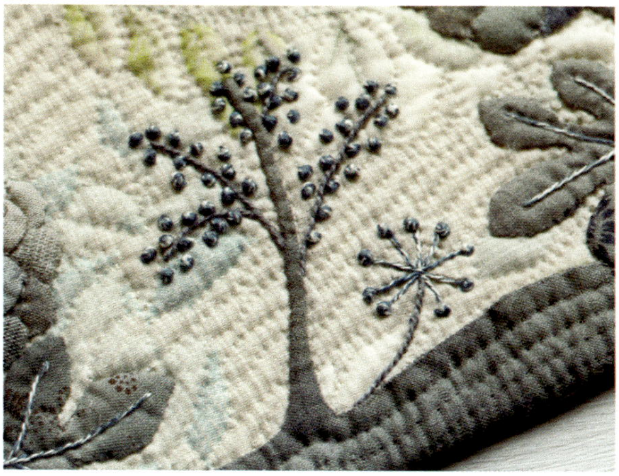

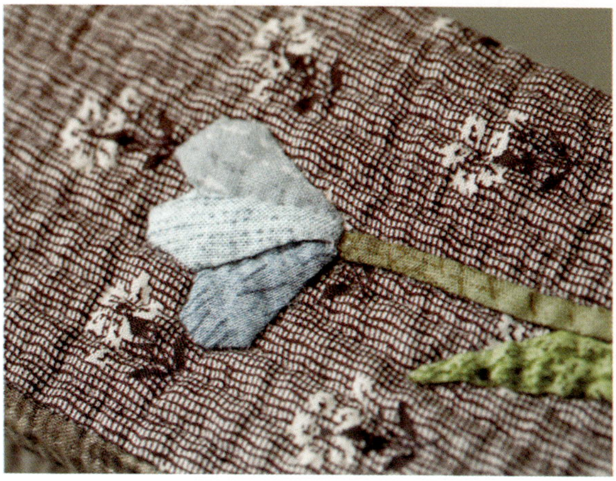

Contents

Tiny Pouches

01	Mini Pouch	6
02	Bluebird Pouch	8
03	Boston Bag Pouch	10
04	Hexagon Pouch	12
05	Triangle Clasp Pouch	14
06	Little Round Pouch	16
07	Tulip Pouch	18
08	See-Through Pouch	20
09	Drawstring Pouch	21

Around the House

10	Tiny Tote	22
11, 12	Bunny Dolls	24
13, 14	Miniature Boxes	26
15	Dragonfly Mini Quilt	28
16	Round Case	30

Convenient Small Items

17	Coin Purse	32
18	Sewing Kit	34
19	Watermelon Pincushions	35
20	Buggy Coin Purse	36
21	Whale Bag	38
22	Tissue Holder	40
23	Glasses Case	41
24	Mobile Phone Case	42
25	Water Bottle Carrier	44
26	Card Case	46

How-To Information

Quiltmaking Basics	48
Making a Pouch	50
Project Instructions	57

Tiny Pouches

01

Mini Pouch

Create a palm-sized pouch in the shape of a shoe, then embellish to make your pouch casual or chic. You'll want to have an entire collection! Instructions begin on page 58.

02

Bluebird Pouch   What are you taking back to your nest, Mr. Bluebird? Add embroidery for the detailed areas. Instructions are on page 59.

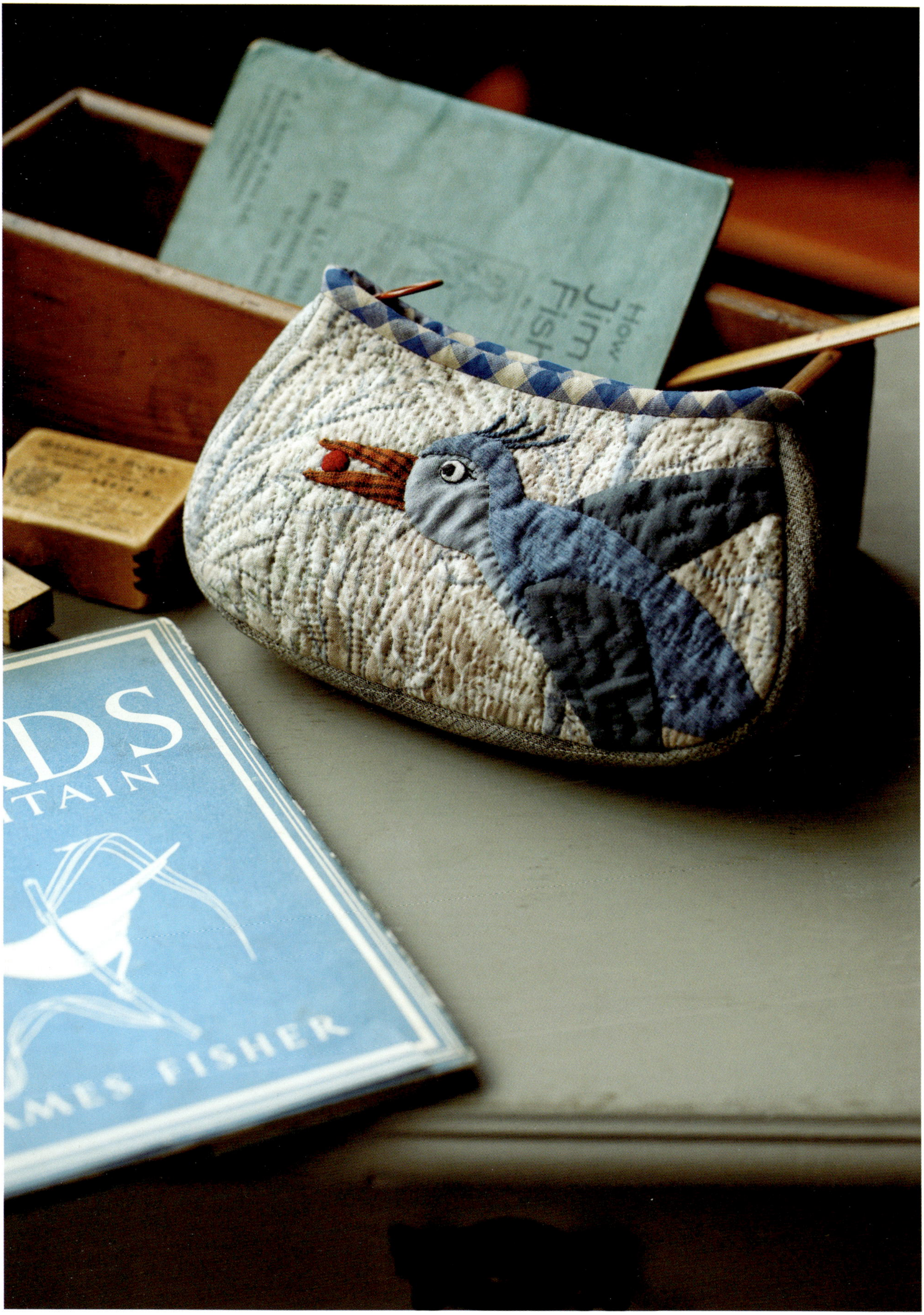
How Jim Fish
DS
TAIN
AMES FISHER

03

Boston Bag Pouch

Make the quilted fabric before using the template to cut out the front and back of the bag. Attach the handles to the gusset. See page 60.

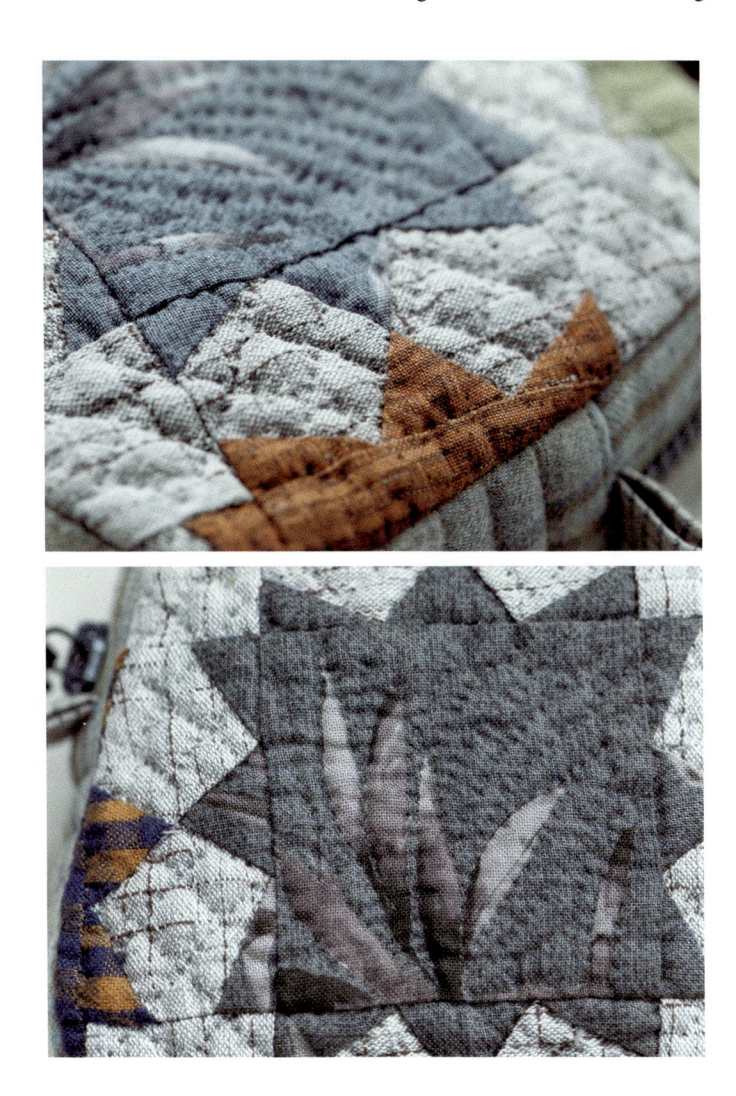

04

Hexagon Pouch   The pale tones of the fabric and the added embroidery give this piece a decidedly feminine touch. See page 50 for instructions.

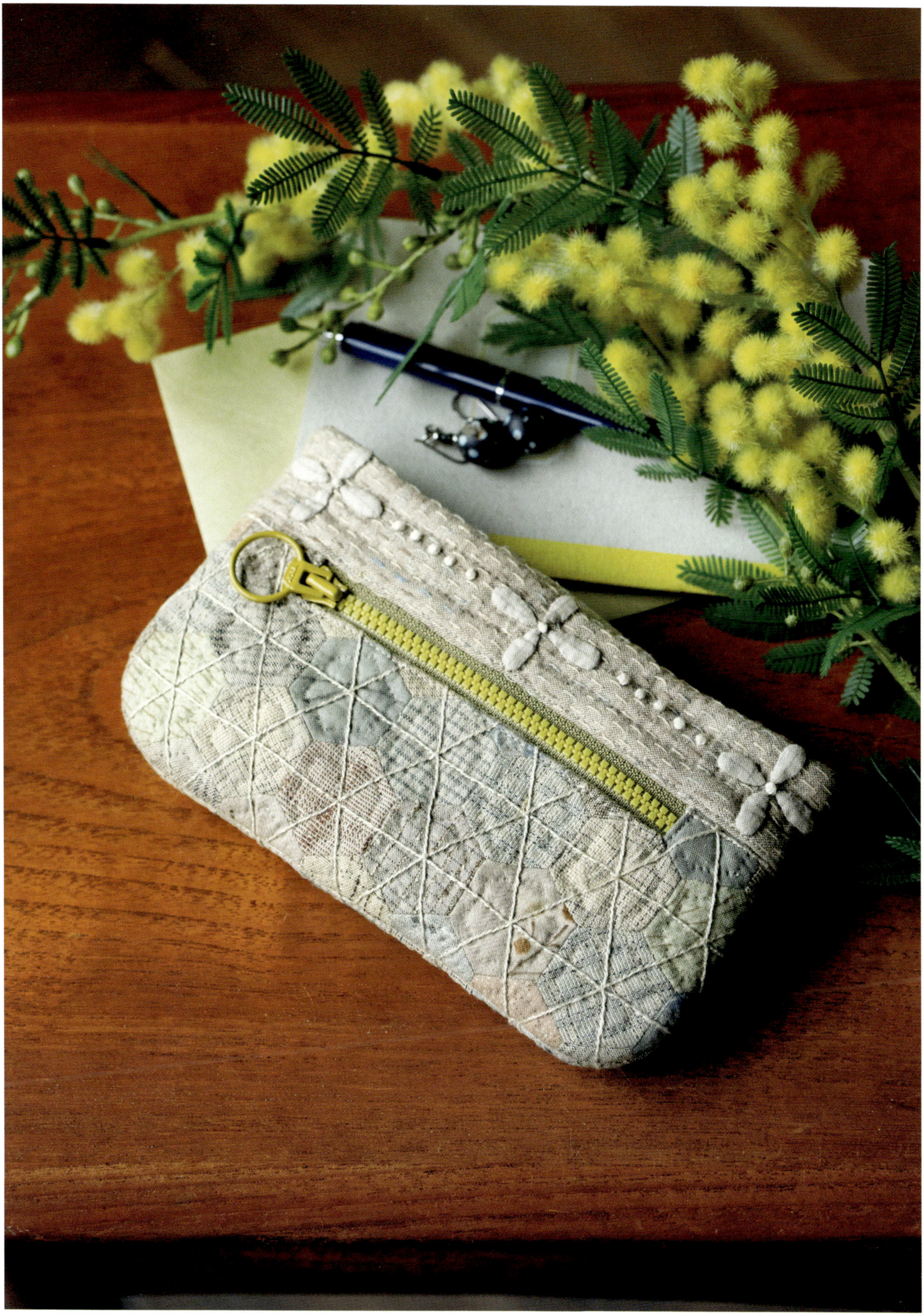

05

Triangle Clasp Pouch   The wide bottom of this pouch makes it useful in so many ways. Stitch together half-square triangles to create the cloth before using the template to cut out the shapes. See page 62.

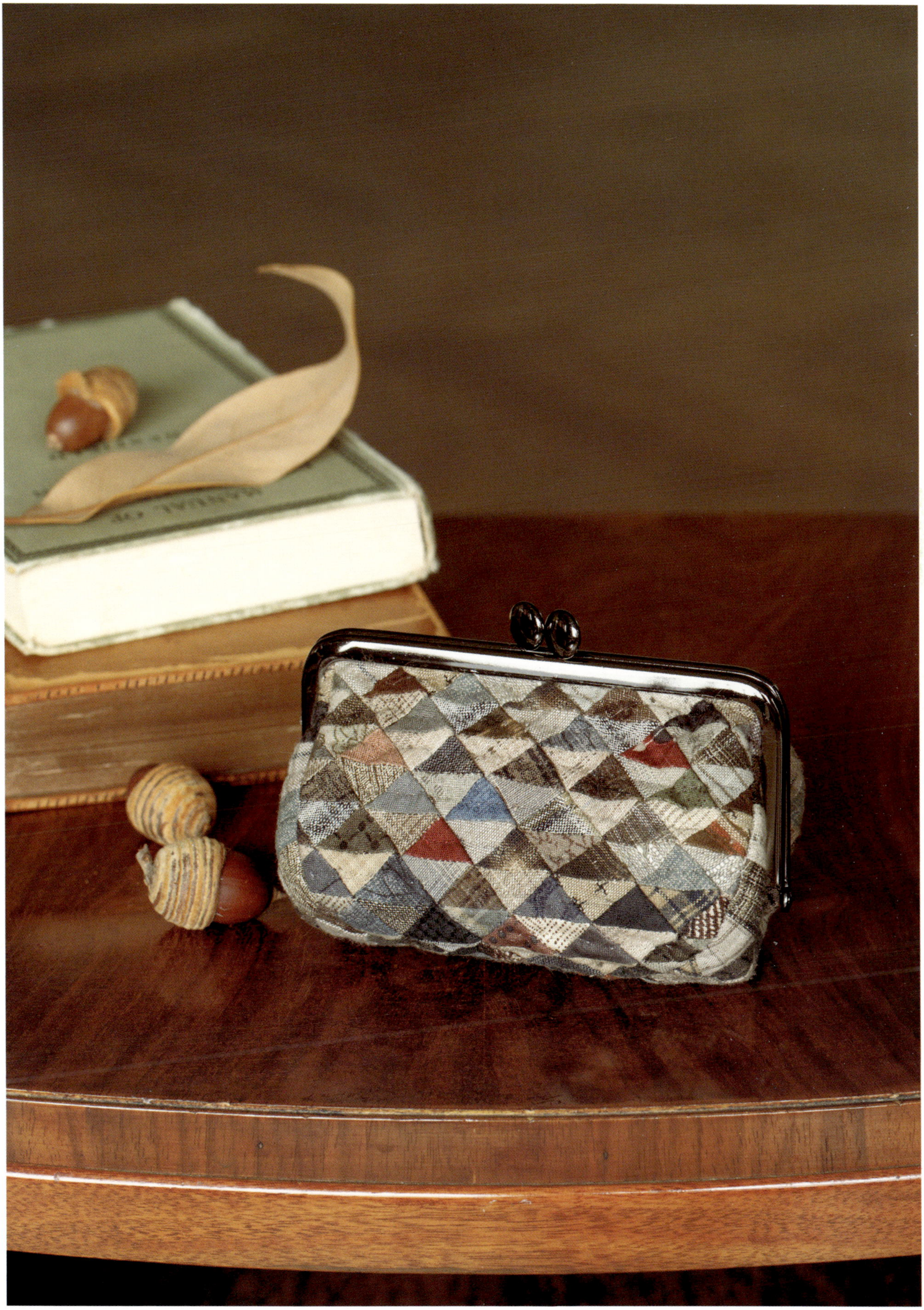

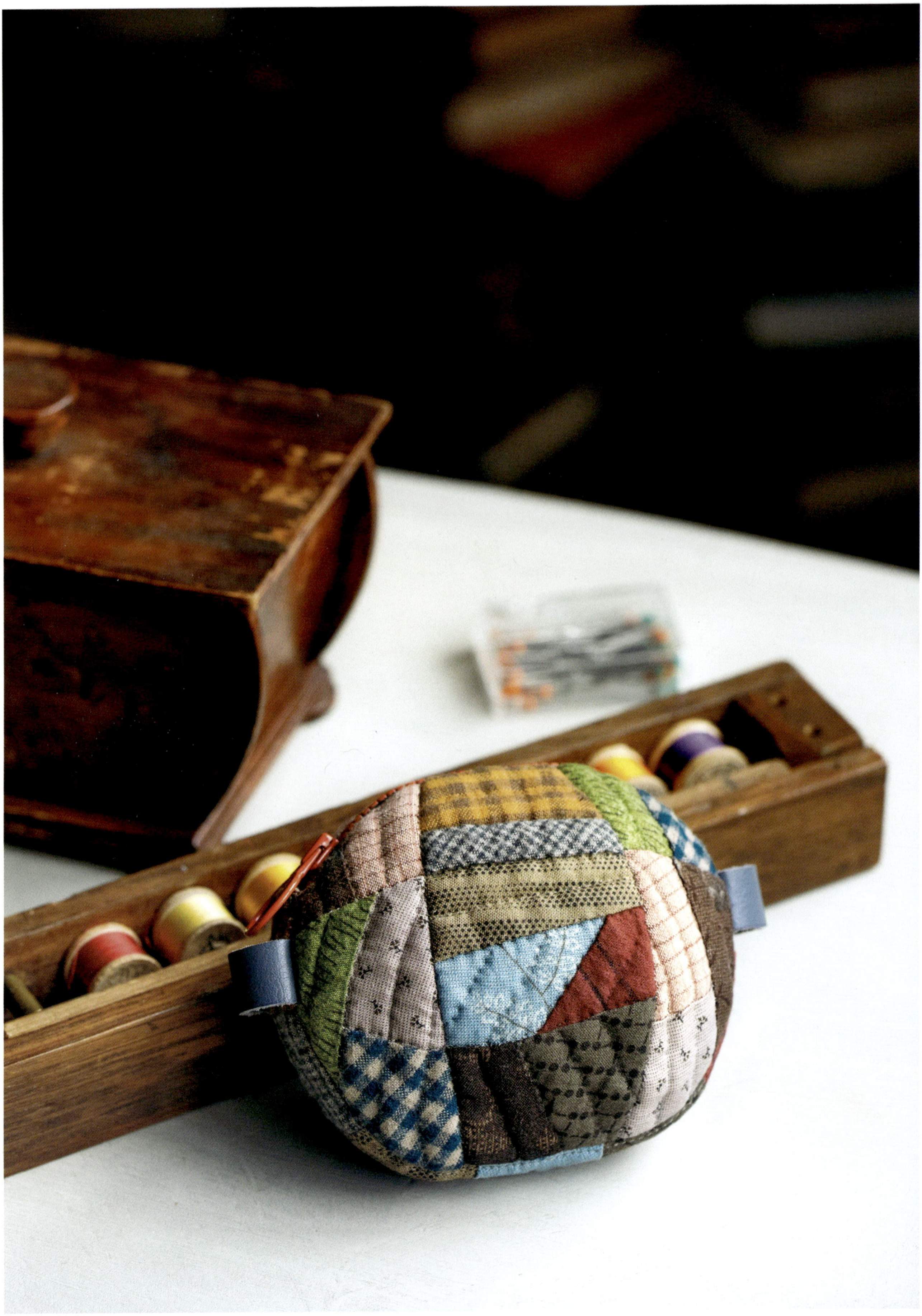

06

Little Round Pouch

I love how adorable a tiny round shape can be.
All kinds of things will fit perfectly inside.
Instructions are on page 64.

07

Tulip Pouch

The tulips are stretching toward the sun, and the breeze is depicted by the quilting lines. It makes me think of a peaceful spring day. See page 66.

08

See-Through Pouch The vinyl front allows you to see not only the contents of the pouch, but also the unexpected appliqué on the inside. See page 68 for instructions.

09

Drawstring Pouch The branches and leaves in the appliqué follow the shape of the pouch. Sew appliquéd leaves to the ends of the drawstring for added cuteness. Instructions begin on page 70.

Around the House 10

Tiny Tote Families are snug in their houses under the twinkling starry sky. The design wraps around the bag, so there's something to see from any angle. See page 72.

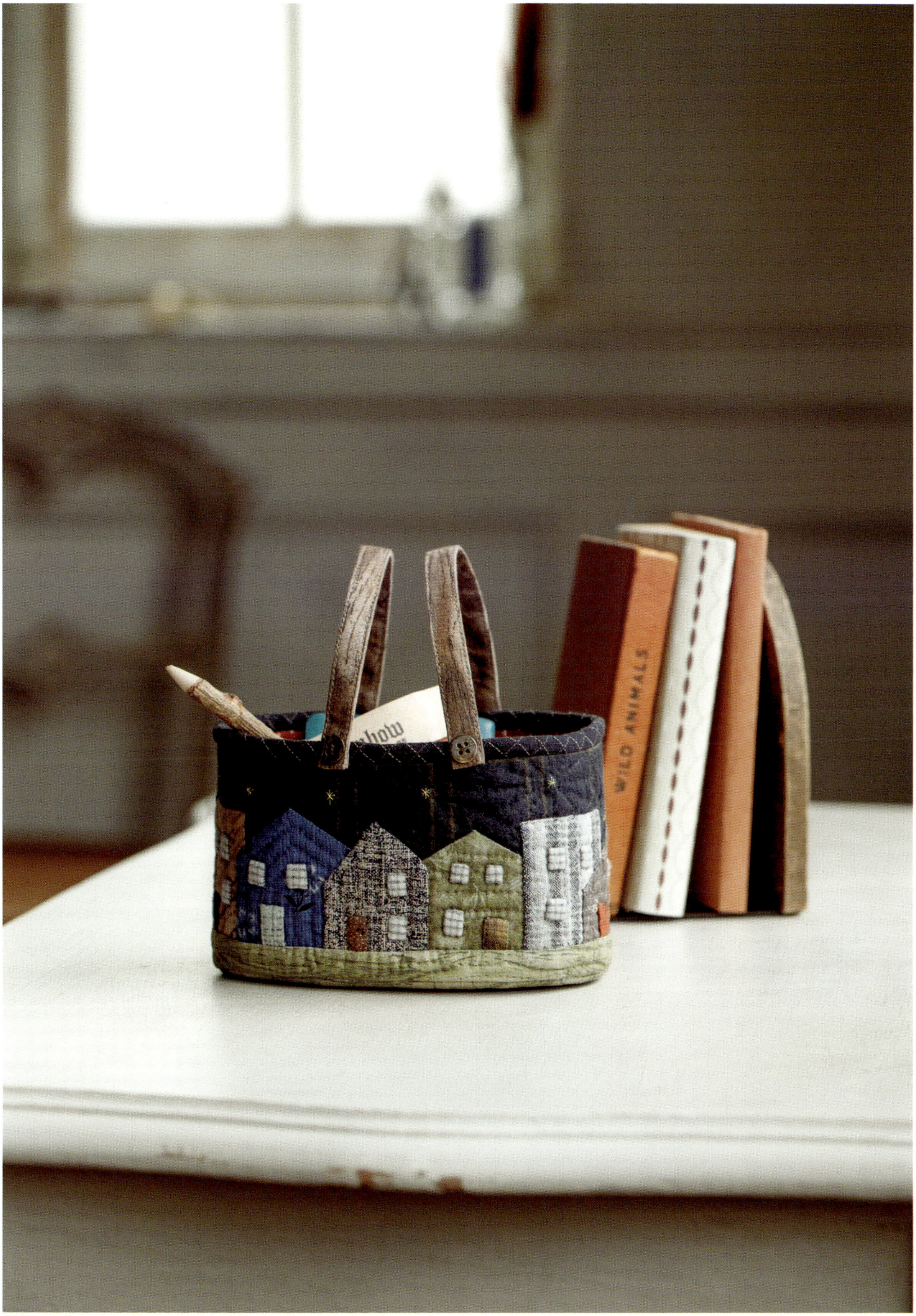
WILD ANIMALS

11, 12

Bunny Dolls   Make a pair of bunny dolls, and customize the clothing for a boy or girl. Even better, make an entire nest of bunny dolls! See page 74.

13, 14

Miniature Boxes   Miniature house-shaped boxes make delightful places for treats and treasures to reside. See page 76.

15

Dragonfly Mini Quilt   Combine appliqué and embroidery to stitch an intricate and stunning mini quilt. See page 79.

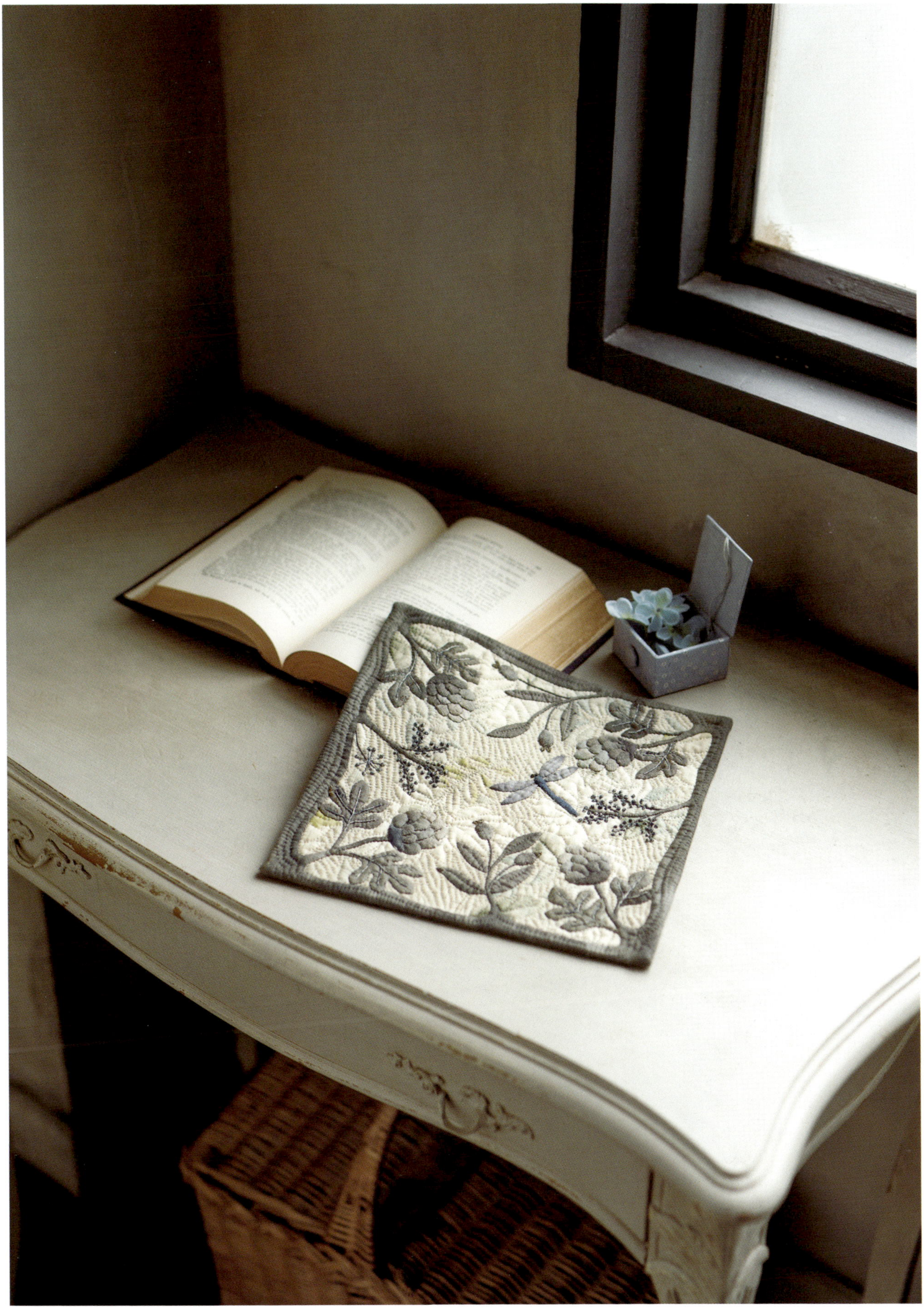

16

Round Case   What will you carry in this round zippered case? Add a touch of whimsy by using a stack of beads in place of handles on the lid. See page 80.

31

Convenient Small Items 17

Coin Purse

I made this design fairly small so that it can easily be tucked into your purse. The magnetic closures keep the coins from spilling out. Instructions are on page 82.

18

Sewing Kit   It's always a good idea to carry a basic sewing kit with you. I designed this one to have extra pockets inside. See page 83.

19

Watermelon Pincushions

Any way you slice it, a watermelon pincushion is a colorful treat. Black button "seeds" add the perfect finishing touch. See page 84.

35

20

Buggy Coin Purse   I like to design fantasy creatures such as this insect with a funny facial expression. It find it useful to carry my coins separately, but you can tuck a bill or two into one side. Instructions are on page 86.

21

Whale Bag

Sea creatures swim across the outside of this small cross-body bag. See page 88.

39

22

Tissue Holder Hide your tissues in plain sight with this beautiful cylindrical holder. Instructions are on page 90.

Glasses Case

The design of this case echoes the shape of a pair of glasses. Customize the appliqué and fabric colors to match your own pair. Instructions are on page 92.

24

Mobile Phone Case

Carry your phone in style with an appliquéd medallion pouch. It's sized large enough to fit most phones. Instructions are on page 94.

25

Water Bottle Carrier The gusset makes this tote perfect for carrying most water bottles. Slip the handles over your wrist for hand-free shopping. See page 96.

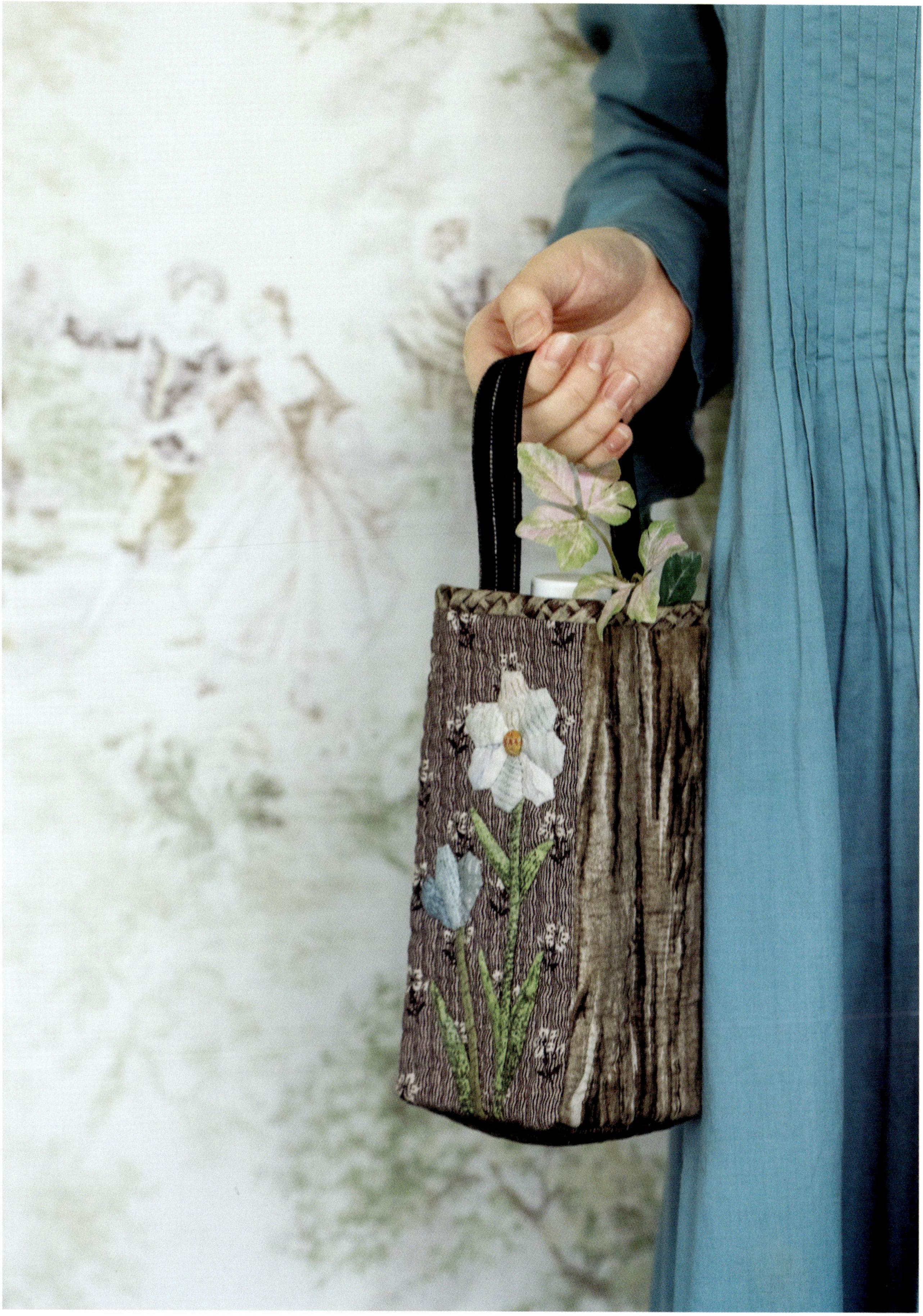

26

Card Case

I believe simple shapes are the easiest to use. The zipper turns the corner to give you plenty of room to get cards in and out.
See page 98.

47

Quiltmaking Basics

Essential Quilting Notions & Tools

The following is a list of basic tools and notions that are useful to have on hand for making quilts.

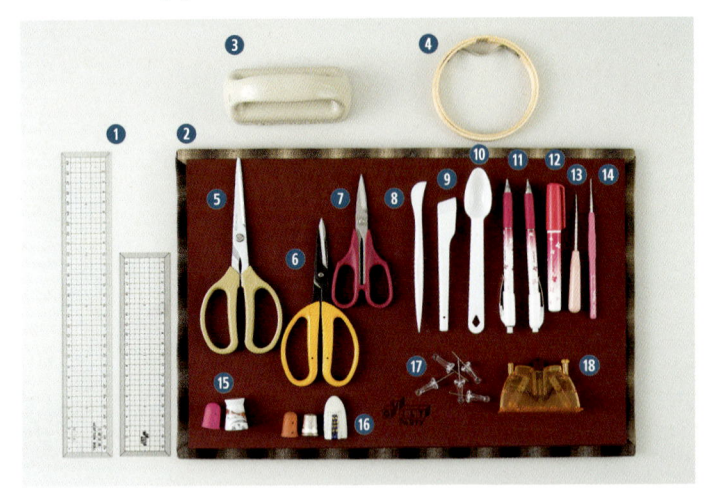

❶ Ruler. Used to trace straight lines when transferring patterns. Rulers with markings made for quilters are useful.
❷ Nonslip Board. Use the nonslip surface board for marking fabric or when using the fabric pressing tool to turn under the seam allowances. The soft side backed with batting and fabric can be used as a mini ironing surface.
❸ Weights (paperweights, beanbags, etc.). Used to weigh down a small quilt when quilting.
❹ Embroidery Hoop. Used to secure fabric when doing embroidery.
❺ Fabric scissors.
❻ Paper scissors.
❼ Thread scissors. All scissors will last longer if you use them for specific tasks, such as fabric, paper, or thread.
❽ Appliqué Hera Marker. Used when working with appliqué pieces. The curved area is particularly useful to help turn under edges of appliqués.
❾ Seam Pressing Tool. Used to press seam allowances down, in lieu of ironing.
❿ Spoon. Often used when pin basting a quilt. Diaper pins are easy to use for this method.
⓫ Marking Pencils. Used to transfer patterns to either paper or fabric or for marking quilting lines. Mechanical pencils allow for greater precision, and lines disappear with water.
⓬ Glue Stick. Used to temporarily hold fabric in place in lieu of pins or basting.
⓭ Awl. To mark corner points when transferring and drawing patterns or to punch holes into leather or suede.
⓮ Extra-fine Awl. Typically a finer tip than a standard awl.
⓯ Thimbles. Used to protect your fingers while quilting. The Rubber Thimble fits under the Porcelain Thimble to keep it from slipping.
⓰ Thimbles. Used to protect your fingers while quilting. The Metal Thimble is for pushing a needle through cloth when quilting. The Leather Thimble fits under another thimble to keep it from slipping.
⓱ Push Pins. Useful to keep layers from shifting when getting ready to baste the quilting sandwich. The longer the pin the better.
⓲ Needle Threader. A simple tool making it easier to thread needles.

Pins & Needles

Use each according to their purpose.

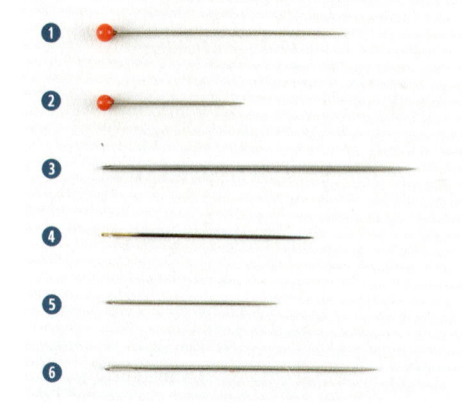

❶ Straight Pin. An easy-to-use long pin with a small head.
❷ Appliqué Pin. A short pin with a small head that won't get in the way while you appliqué.
❸ Basting Needle. A long needle for basting.
❹ Sharps, Appliqué, or Piecing Needle. Easy to appliqué with, as they tend to bend with use. Used to piece together fabric.
❺ Quilting Betweens Needles. Shorter than sharps; used for quilting.
❻ Embroidery Needles. With a large eye to handle the number of threads for stitchery.

Batting

Batting is a layer of insulation that lies between the top and backing/lining of a quilt or quilted project. Often made of cotton, wool, bamboo, or other material, batting can be fairly thin or very lofty. I usually use a medium-loft batting for bed quilts, while using thin batting for projects that use trapunto. Do not use fusible batting if you plan to hand quilt, as it is hard to push the needles through. For small items, such as in this book, I tend to use a medium loft, but you should use what you most like.

❶ Cotton Batting.
❷ Fusible Batting.
❸ Fusible Interfacing.

Useful Notions for Small Projects

Here are recommended parts that not only offer utility but also add highlights to your projects.

Zippers

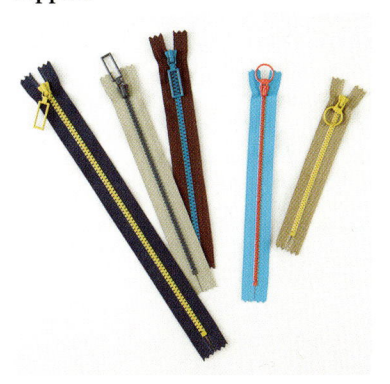

Colorful zippers can be an important part of the design. I try to choose easy-to-use zippers while giving consideration to the zipper tapes, teeth, and pull. I like zippers with a large pull.

16 Round Case
page 30

For this cylindrical accessory case, I chose a zipper with a large pull for easy opening. I coordinated the project with a chic slate blue zipper.

Free-Style Zippers

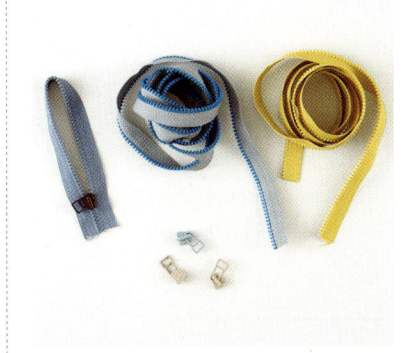

This type of zipper allows you to adjust the length to your liking. You can also use two zipper tapes in different colors. Being able to select a zipper pull also adds to the fun of coordinating colors.

20 Buggy Coin Purse
page 36

One free-style zipper tape is folded in half and goes all around the purse opening. The zipper pull stops before the loop.

Metal Purse Clasps

There are various types of metal clasps, so be sure to look for a design that you like. They come in different sizes, so adjust the size of your project according to the metal clasps used.

24 Mobile Phone Case   page 42 (left)

18 Sewing Kit   page 34 (right)

Both projects use the same size metal clasps but in different colors.

Magnetic Closures

Magnetic closures are useful to close a bag opening or hold a lid closed. Unlike zippers, magnetic closures are easy to install because they can be attached on the outside at the last step. The magnetic closures on the left are in standard size. The ones on the right are small, like buttons, and used in Project 17. I wrapped the magnetic closures with fabric before attaching them. In this way, they blend in with the background fabric and do not stand out even if they are made of a different material.

17 Coin Purse
page 32

Grommets

Normally, grommets are attached to a bag to thread bag handles. I used a grommet for an opening of the tissue holder in this book.

22 Tissue Holder
page 40

I used a clear grommet so it does not stand out. Installing a grommet is easy. You just need to make a hole and insert the grommet by hand.

49

Making a Pouch

Even small pouches have many parts. There are a few tricks you can use to complete them neatly. On the pages that follow, we will use the steps for creating Project 04 to introduce those tricks.

04

Project page 12   Full-size templates on page 56

Hexagon Pouch

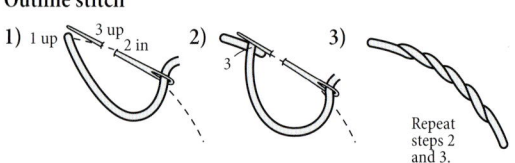

Pouch front A: Cut 1 piece each for the top, batting, and backing/divider fabric.

- 3 cm [1¼"]
- Appliqué
- 5 cm [2"]
- tab positions
- colonial knot (1 strand)
- Outline quilt.
- Quilt every 1 cm [⅜"].
- 12 cm [4¾"] zipper is installed here.
- 18 cm [7⅛"]

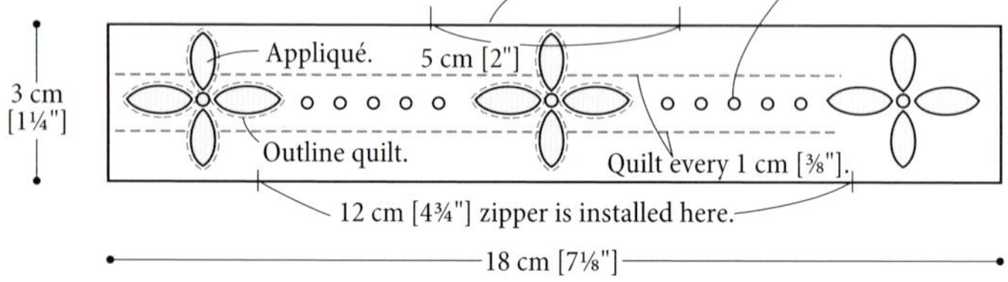

Pouch front B: Cut 1 piece each for the top, batting, and backing/divider fabric.
Divider (use pattern for pouch front B but do not cut out zipper opening): Cut 1 piece from backing/divider fabric.

- outline stitches (2 strands)
- Zipper is installed here.
- 7 cm [2¾"]
- 1.6 cm [⅝"]
- Quilt 0.3 cm [⅛"] from the edge.
- 18 cm [7⅛"]

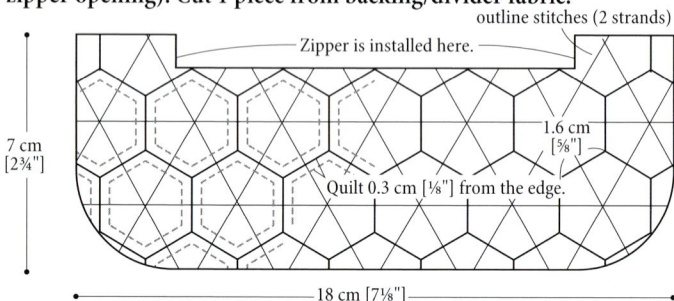

Pouch back: Cut 1 piece each for the top, batting, and backing/divider fabric.

- outline stitches (2 strands)
- 2.2 cm [⅞"] magnetic closure wrapped in fabric
- 10 cm [4"]
- Quilt 0.3 cm [⅛"] from the edge.
- 1.6 cm [⅝"]
- 18 cm [7⅛"]

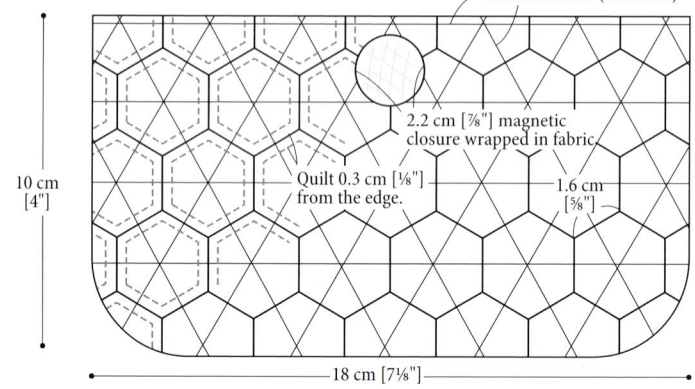

Tab: Cut 1 piece each for the top, batting, backing, and interfacing.

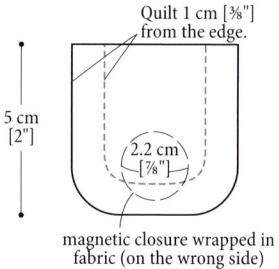

- Quilt 1 cm [⅜"] from the edge.
- 5 cm [2"]
- 2.2 cm [⅞"]
- magnetic closure wrapped in fabric (on the wrong side)
- 5 cm [2"]

Materials Needed

Cottons:
- Assorted fat quarters and scraps for patchwork and appliqués
- Tab and magnetic closure: 15 x 15 cm [6" x 6"]
- Backing and divider: 50 x 25 cm [20" x 10"]
- Bias-cut binding for seams: 2.5 x 60 cm [1" x 24"]

Batting: 40 x 25 cm [16" x 10"]

15 cm [6"] zipper

1 pair sew-on magnetic closure (2.2 cm [⅞"] in diameter)

Interfacing: 8 x 8 cm [3¼" x 3¼"]

Embroidery floss in ecru

Candlewick thread or perle cotton

Colonial knot

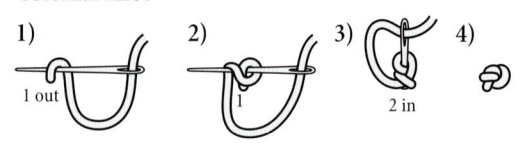

1) 1 out
2) 1
3)
4) 2 in

Outline stitch

1) 1 up   3 up   2 in
2) 3
3) Repeat steps 2 and 3.

- Do not add seam allowances when cutting interfacing. When cutting backing, add 1.5 cm [⅝"] seam allowances. Cut hexagon pieces with 0.7 cm [¼"] seam allowances. When cutting appliqués, add 0.3 to 0.4 cm [⅛"] seam allowances. Cut all other pieces with 1 cm [⅜"] seam allowances.
- Piece together the hexagons and cut to make the pouch front B top and pouch back top.
- Stitch appliqués and embroidery designs on the pouch front A.

Preparing Fabric

1 Gather your materials. In this example, we omitted embroideries and piecing, so we chose fabric that did not need to be sewn together or appliquéd. As for the zipper, we will use a 15 cm long zipper that is easily available. We will cut and adjust its length according to the zipper opening.

2 Cut out individual fabric pieces, adding the necessary seam allowances. (For the actual project, the pouch front and back are made by piecing hexagons together.)

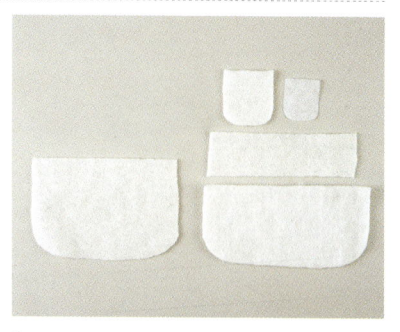

3 Prepare batting and interfacing. Use batting for areas that will be hand quilted. Use fusible batting for parts that will be machine sewn or machine quilted.

Making the Pouch Front   Red thread is used to make seams stand out in these photos.

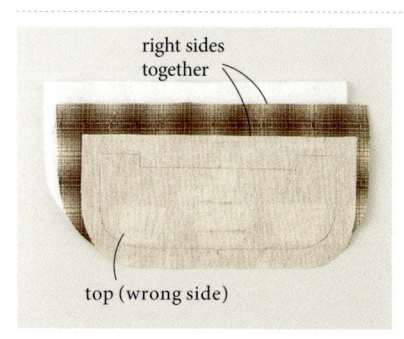

4 Layer the batting, backing, and top for front B together, placing the backing and top right sides together. (To make the actual top for Project 04, we would piece hexagons together and stitch the embroideries.)

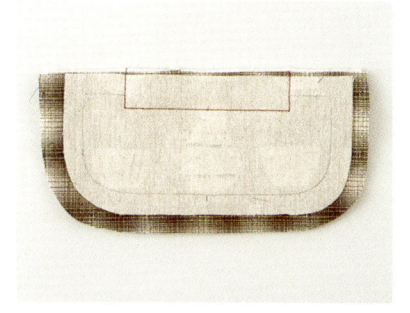

5 Machine sew around where the zipper will be installed. As shown in the photo, stitch beyond the marks at the start and end.

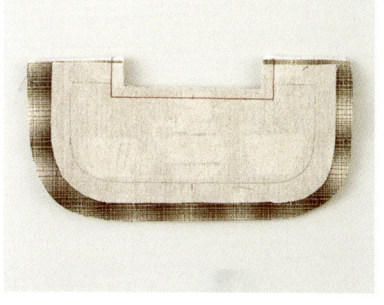

6 Trim away excess fabric to 0.7 cm [¼"] from the seam sewn in step 5.

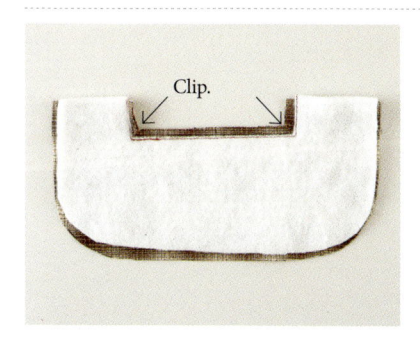

7 Flip over the piece, and trim away batting close to the seam. Clip into the seam allowance on the corners of the backing and top.

8 Flip over the top right side out, and smooth out the zipper opening.

9 Baste and quilt. The piece in the photo was machine quilted. The piece in Project 04 was hand quilted.

51

10 Put a 15 cm [5⅞"] long zipper along the zipper opening, and mark the zipper tape. Align the left edge of the zipper opening with the 0.5 cm [scant ¼"] mark from the zipper slider, and mark at the 12 cm [4¾"] point (width of the zipper opening).

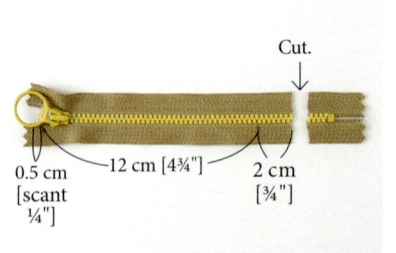

11 Add 2 cm [¾"] to the 12 cm [4¾"] mark, and cut the zipper.

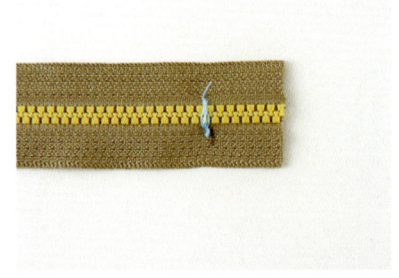

12 Sew along the mark made in step 10. (Normally, we use thread in a color that blends in with the zipper teeth.)

13 Put the zipper and pouch body together, and machine sew.

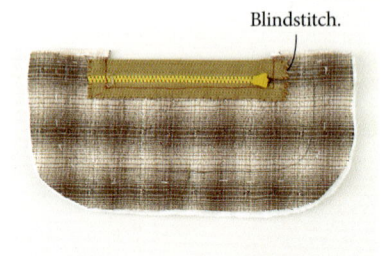

14 Blindstitch the zipper tapes down to the backing.

15 Next add the divider.

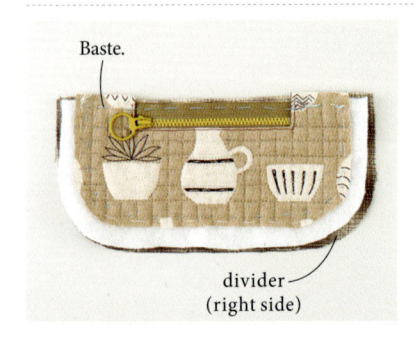

16 Put the pouch front and divider together, and baste all around to temporarily sew pieces together.

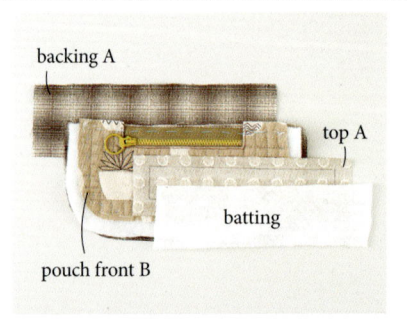

17 Sandwich the pouch front B with the top, batting, and backing for pouch front A.

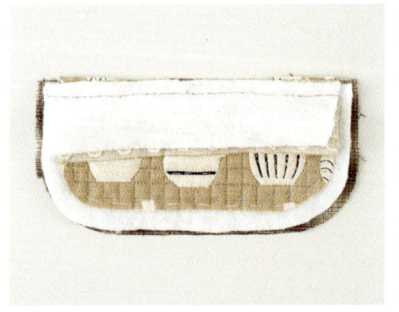

18 Machine sew.

52

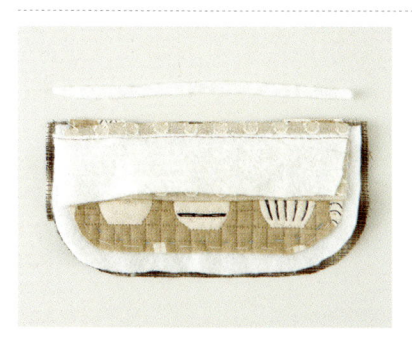

19 Trim away the batting only, close to the seam.

20 Turn pouch front A right side out, and edgestitch.

21 Quilt pouch front A. Here I added straight line quilting every 1 cm [⅜"].

Making the Pouch Back

22 Put the top for the pouch back, batting, and backing together, and quilt. In this photo, we machine quilted a lattice pattern.

Wrapping the Magnetic Closure with Fabric

23 Cut a 3.8 cm [1.5"] circle of fabric. Sew running stitches along the outer edges of the fabric, and insert the magnetic closure in the middle. Pull up the thread and tie securely. Repeat with the remaining half of the magnetic closure.

Making a Tab

24 Prepare the top, backing, and batting for the tab. Fuse the interfacing on the wrong side of the backing.

25 Put the pieces right sides together, and sew along the edges.

26 Trim away excess batting close to the seam, and turn right side out. Topstitch with a sewing machine.

Putting the Pouch Front and Back Together

27 Put the pouch front and back right sides together.

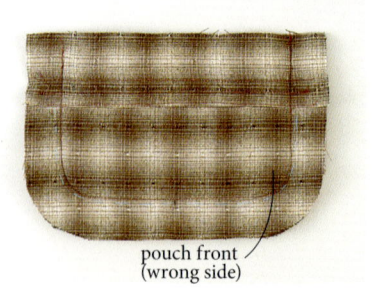

28 Baste to temporarily secure in place, then machine sew.

29 Put the fabric strip to bind the seam allowances on the pouch front, and sew along the edges.

30 Trim away the excess seam allowances.

31 Bind the seam allowances, and blindstitch down to the pouch back. Since the pouch front contains the divider, I pressed the seam allowances to the pouch back.

Attaching the Tab

32 Turn the pouch right side out, and mark the center. Match the center with the center of the tab, and pin the tab in place.

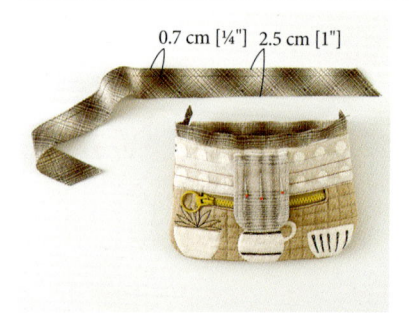

33 Layer the tab, and put the fabric strip to bind the seam allowances along the pouch opening.

34 Baste, then machine sew along the pouch opening.

35 Trim away the excess seam allowances to 0.7 cm [¼"].

36 Bind the seam allowances, and blindstitch down to the backing.

37 Turn the pouch right side out. Blindstitch the wrapped magnetic closure to the tab and pouch back.

38 Now your pouch is complete!

This is what the actual project looks like:

front

back

Yoko's Voice

Advice on making small projects

When I make small projects, I think about how to put pieces together when I design them. I consider structures, such as how to bind seam allowances, and how to attach zippers and other parts, and decide on the design so as to create beautiful projects more efficiently. Many failures and experiences I have encountered up until now are useful in making such decisions: "I tried that way to make a beautiful project," or "I tried this way and my project did not turn out right." I have made many small projects and bags in the past. Having a pool of knowledge and memories helps me make decisions on the spot.

If I still have doubts, I just sew the pieces together to see how they come together. Sometimes this goes well, and other times I start all over again. There are no shortcuts to creating projects. I hope you will patiently continue sewing and allow your hands to develop a feel for it.

55

04 Hexagon Pouch

Pouch back (Cut 1.)
Cut out the entire shape of pouch front A and B to make the pouch back.

Pouch front A (Cut 1.)

zipper opening area

Pouch front B (Cut 1.)

Divider (Cut 1.)
Do not cut out the zipper opening area on the divider.

Hexagon (Cut 67.)

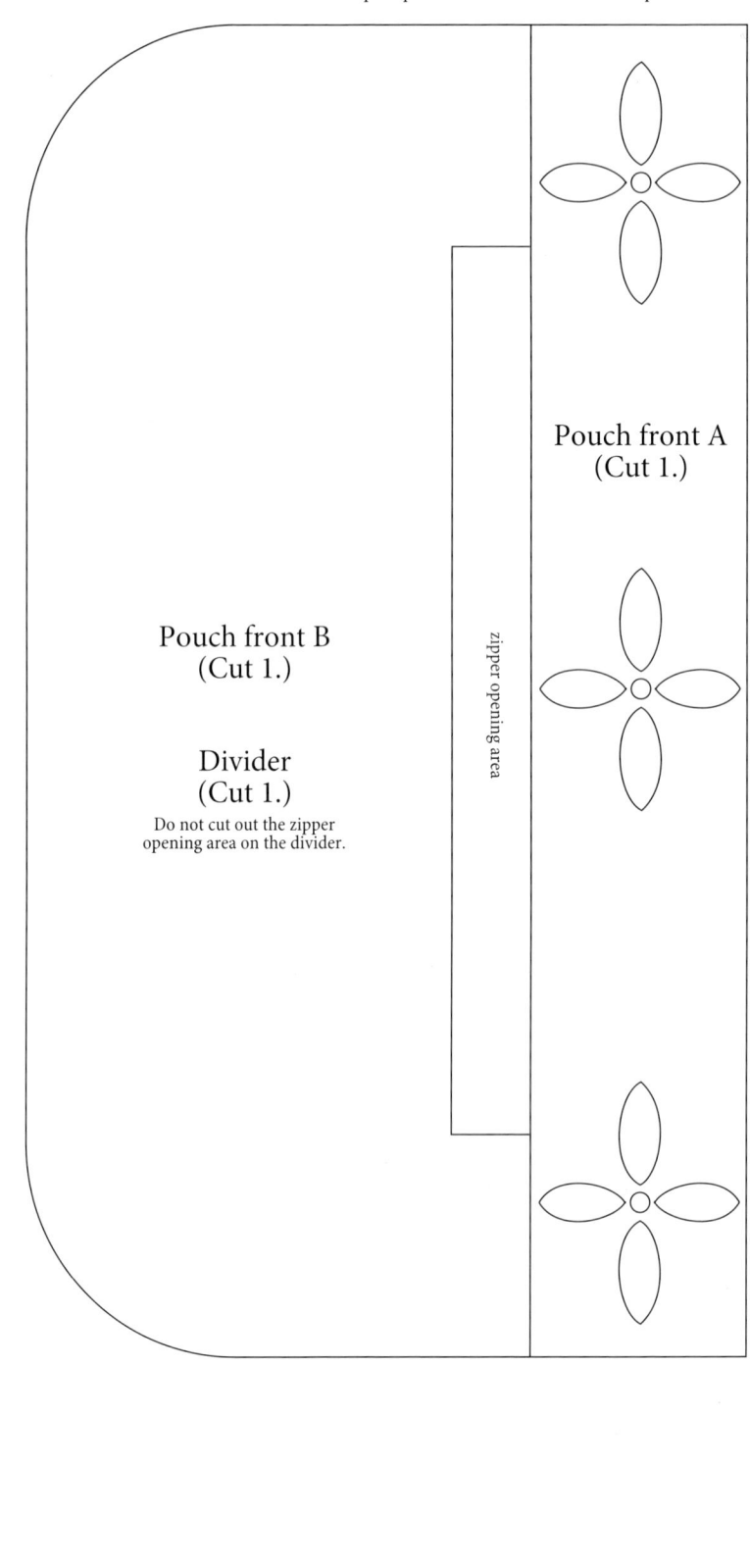

Tab (Cut 1.)

Project
INSTRUCTIONS

- All measurements listed for the following projects are in centimeters (cm) and in inches [in brackets].

- Seam allowances must be added; see each pattern for specific information for each piece. Add 0.3 to 0.5 cm [⅛" to scant ¼"] for appliqué, 0.7 cm [¼"] for piecing.

- The dimensions of the finished projects are shown in the drawings.

- Note that the quilted pieces tend to shrink somewhat, depending on the type of fabric used, the thickness of the batting, the amount of quilting, and individual quilting technique. Double-check your quilted pieces against the pattern dimensions.

For portions of the projects, as well as the quilting, you can use a sewing machine. However, all projects can be made by hand. If sewing by hand, use a backstitch.

01 Mini Pouch

Project page 6　Full-size templates on page 99

Materials Needed

Cottons:
- Background fabric: 30 x 15 cm [12" x 6"]
- Solid white for appliqués: 15 x 15 cm [6" x 6"]
- Tab: 4.5 x 4.5 cm [1¾" x 1¾"]
- Backing: 35 x 15 cm [14" x 6"]
- Bias-cut binding for seams: 2.5 x 15 cm [1" x 6"]

Batting: 35 x 15 cm [14" x 6"]
20 cm [8"] zipper
1 cm [⅜"] wide D-ring
Embroidery floss in various colors

Instructions

1 Referring to the diagram above right and the full-size template on page 99, stitch appliqués to the background and embroider to make the pouch body top.

2 Layer the prepared top with backing and batting (figure 1). Sew along the pouch opening, turn right side out, and quilt.

3 Insert the zipper (figure 2). Sew the pouch bottom, then use the excess backing to bind the seam allowances.

4 Sew the tab between the pouch body pieces; use the bias fabric to bind the seam allowances.

5 Sew the gusset.

Pouch body: Cut 1 piece each for the top, batting, and backing.

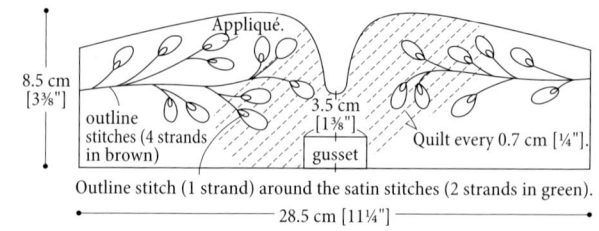

- When cutting appliqués, add 0.3 to 0.4 cm [⅛"] seam allowances. When cutting backing, add 1.5 cm [⅝"] seam allowances to the bottom edge. Cut all other edges and pieces with 1 cm [⅜"] seam allowances.
- Stitch appliqués and embroidery designs on the pouch body top.

Tab: Cut 1 piece.

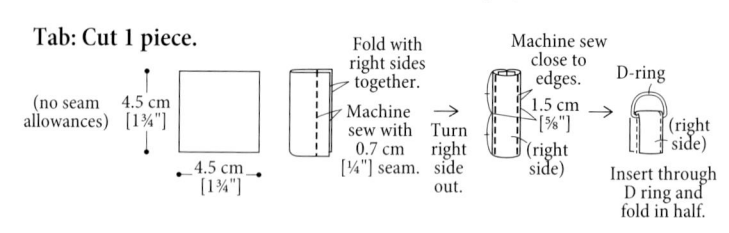

Figure 1: Assembling the pouch

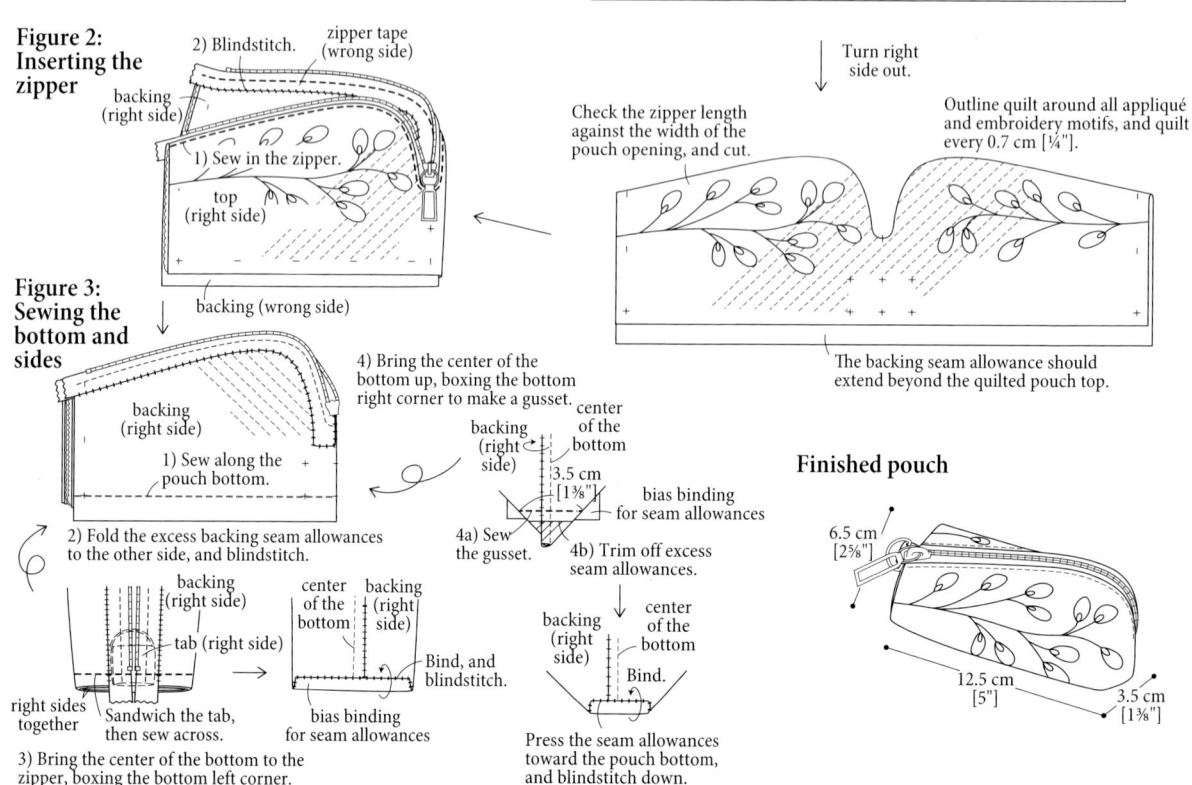

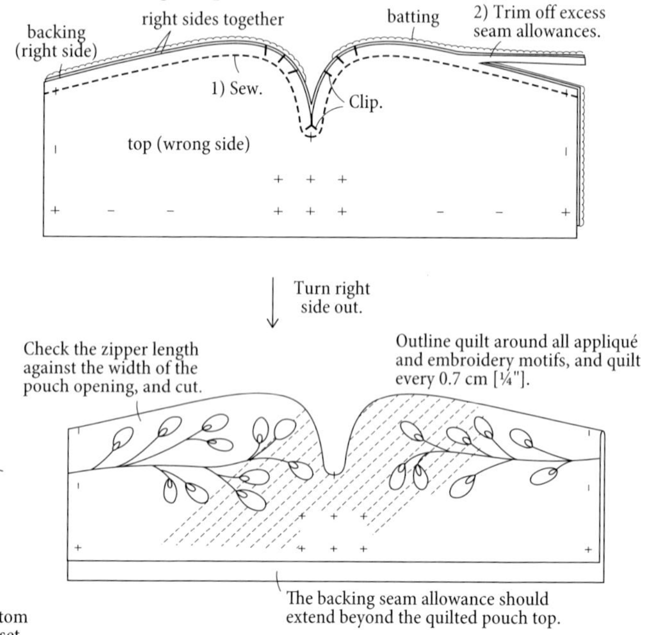

Figure 2: Inserting the zipper

Figure 3: Sewing the bottom and sides

Finished pouch

6.5 cm [2⅝"]
12.5 cm [5"]
3.5 cm [1⅜"]

02

Project page 8   Full-size templates on page 100

Bluebird Pouch

Materials Needed
Cottons:
- Background print: 35 x 25 cm [14" x 10"]
- Assorted fat quarters and scraps for appliqués
- Yarn-dyed plaid for gusset and pouch bottom: 50 x 20 cm [20" x 8"]
- Backing: 50 x 40 cm [20" x 16"]
- Blue check for binding: 3.5 x 40 cm [1⅜" x 16"]

Batting: 50 x 40 cm [20" x 16"]
Low-loft fusible batting: 45 x 5 cm [18" x 2"]
15 cm [6"] zipper; shorten to fit (5⅞")
Embroidery floss in various colors

Instructions
1 Referring to the diagram above right and the full-size template on page 100, stitch appliqués on the background and embroider to make the pouch front top.
2 Layer the pouch front top, pouch back top, and gusset/pouch bottom top individually with batting and backing.
3 Put the pouch front/back and gusset/bottom right sides together matching centers (indicated by stars); sew along the sides. Fold the excess backing seam allowances over the seams and blindstitch in place to bind (figure 1).
4 Use bias-cut binding to attach the zipper to the pouch opening (figure 2).

Pouch front/back: Cut 2 pieces each for the top, batting, and backing.

Quilt following the pattern of the fabric.
outline stitches (4 strands in blue)
appliqués
11.2 cm [4⅜"]
satin stitches (2 strands in black)
outline stitches around the eye (1 strand in black)
(Stitch appliqués and embroideries on the pouch front only.)
20.2 cm [8"]

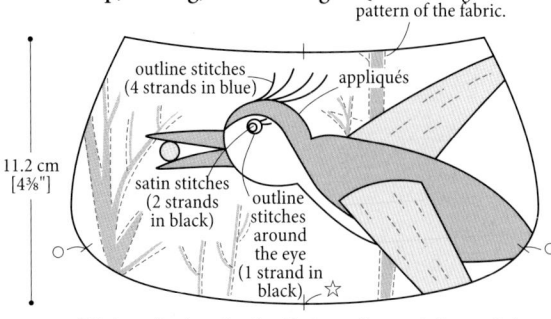

Gusset/pouch bottom: Cut 1 piece each for the top, fusible batting, and backing.

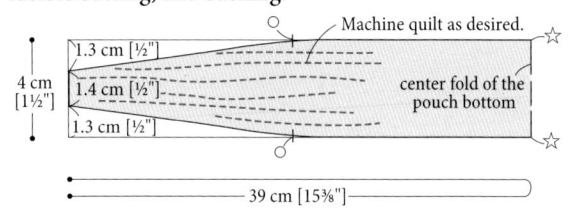

Machine quilt as desired.
4 cm [1½"]
1.3 cm [½"]
1.4 cm [½"]
1.3 cm [½"]
center fold of the pouch bottom
39 cm [15⅜"]

- When cutting appliqués, add 0.3 to 0.4 cm [⅛"] seam allowances. When cutting backing for the gusset/pouch bottom only, add 1.5 cm [⅝"] seam allowances. Cut all other pieces with 1 cm [⅜"] seam allowances.
- When cutting binding, cut on bias.
- Stitch appliqués and embroidery designs on the pouch front top.
- Make a quilt sandwich with top, batting, and backing; quilt.

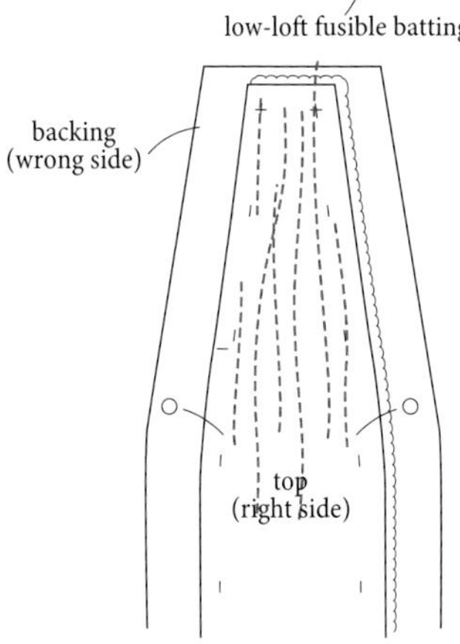

Figure 1: Assembling the pouch

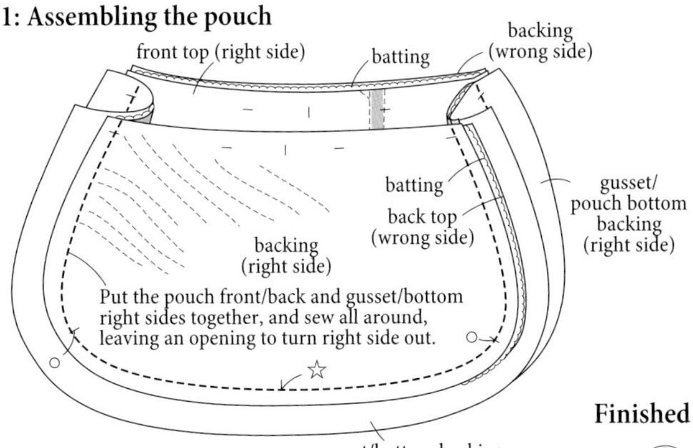

front top (right side)
batting
backing (wrong side)
batting
back top (wrong side)
backing (right side)
gusset/pouch bottom backing (right side)
Put the pouch front/back and gusset/bottom right sides together, and sew all around, leaving an opening to turn right side out.
gusset/bottom backing (wrong side)

Figure 2: Sew in the zipper

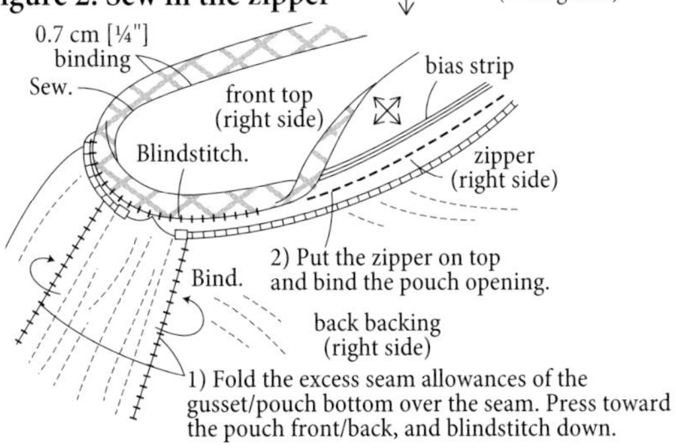

0.7 cm [¼"] binding
Sew.
Blindstitch.
front top (right side)
bias strip
zipper (right side)
Bind.
back backing (right side)
1) Fold the excess seam allowances of the gusset/pouch bottom over the seam. Press toward the pouch front/back, and blindstitch down.
2) Put the zipper on top and bind the pouch opening.

low-loft fusible batting
backing (wrong side)
top (right side)

Finished pouch

11.9 cm [4¾"]
20.2 cm [8"]
4 cm [1½"]

59

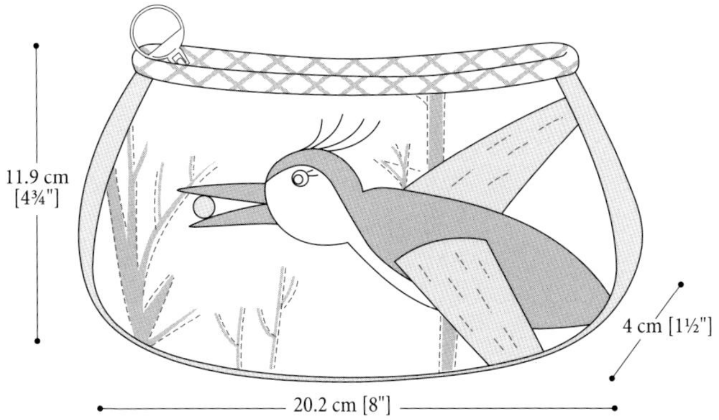

03

Project page 10
Full-size templates on page 61

Boston Bag Pouch

Materials Needed

Cottons:
- Assorted fat quarters and scraps for patchwork, handles, and tab
- Plaid for gusset: 50 x 20 cm [20" x 8"]
- Print for pouch back: 50 x 20 cm [20" x 8"]
- Backing: 50 x 40 cm [20" x 16"]
- Bias-cut binding for seams: 2.5 x 100 cm [1" x 40"]

Batting: 50 x 40 cm [20" x 16"]
Interfacing: 5 x 18 cm [2" x 7"]
18 cm [7"] zipper

Instructions

1 Referring to the diagram above right and the full-size templates on page 61, stitch patchwork pieces together to make the pouch front top.
2 Layer the patchwork piece with batting and backing; quilt. Cut out, adding 1 cm [⅜"] seam allowances.
3 Layer the pouch back top with batting and backing. Quilt as desired.
4 Prepare the handles and tabs (figures 1 and 2).
5 Sew the zipper between the zipper gusset pieces; baste the tabs onto both ends of the zipper (figure 3).
6 Layer the pouch bottom top with batting and backing, sandwiching the zipper gusset as shown in figure 3. Sew at each end and turn right side out. Quilt as desired.

Pouch front: Cut 1 piece each for the top, batting, and backing.

After quilting, add seam allowances to the finished (sewing) line, and trim.

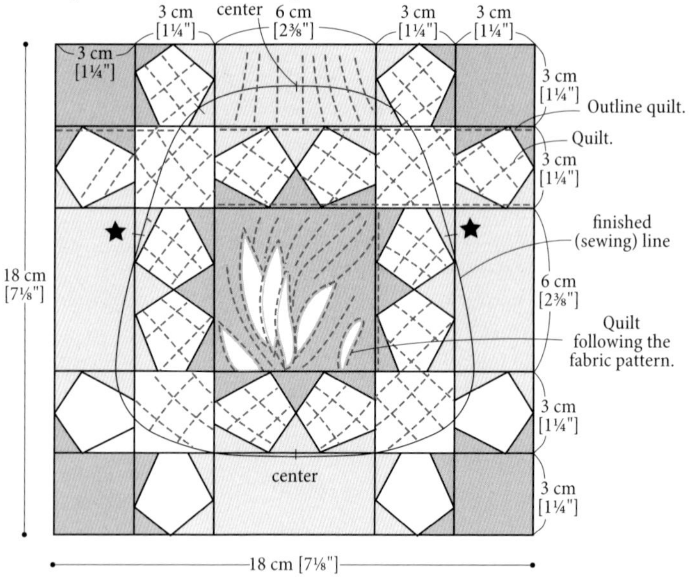

- Cut patchwork pieces with 0.7 cm [¼"] seam allowances. Do not add seam allowances when cutting handles or tabs. Cut all other pieces with 1 cm [⅜"] seam allowances.
- Piece together shapes to make blocks and then join blocks.
- Make a quilt sandwich with top, batting, and backing; machine quilt. Cut to make pouch front top.

Zipper gusset: Cut 2 each from plaid, batting, and batting.

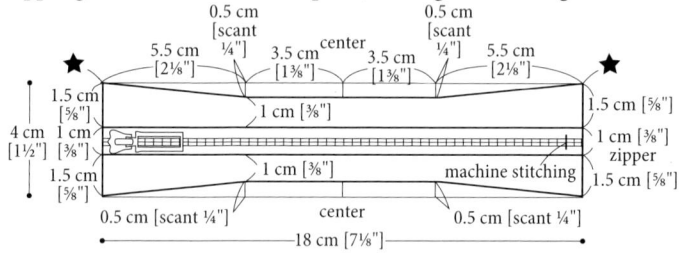

Cut the zipper teeth to 17.5 cm [6⅞"], and stitch with sewing machine.

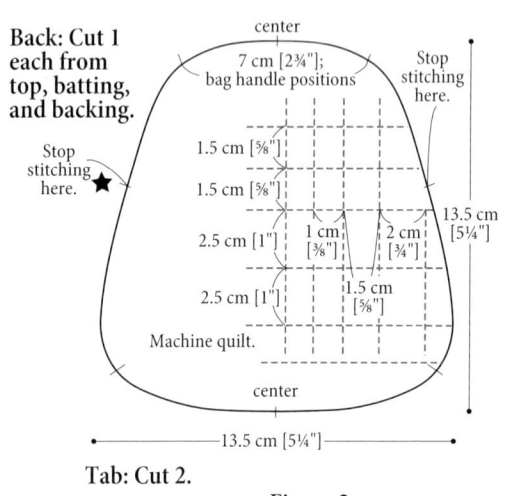

Pouch bottom/gusset: Cut 1 each from top, batting, and backing.

Back: Cut 1 each from top, batting, and backing.

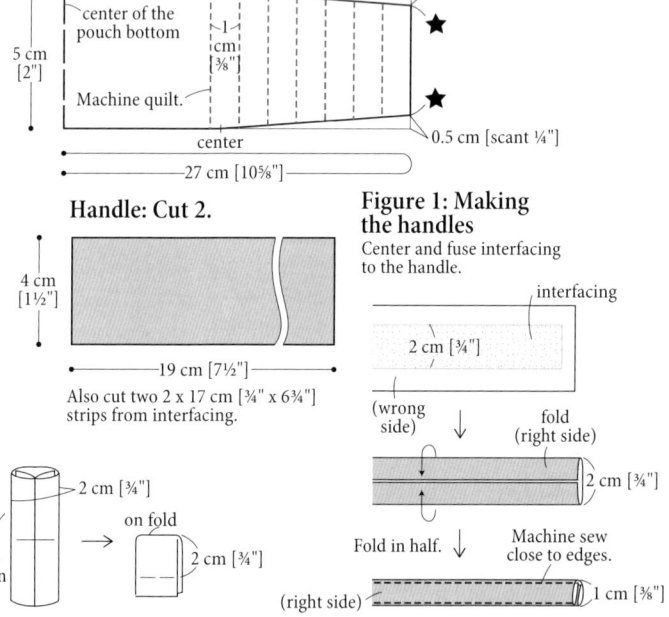

Handle: Cut 2.

Also cut two 2 x 17 cm [¾" x 6¾"] strips from interfacing.

Tab: Cut 2.

Figure 1: Making the handles

Center and fuse interfacing to the handle.

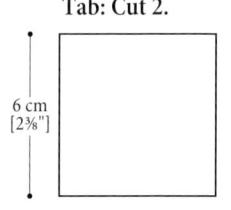

Figure 2: Making the tabs

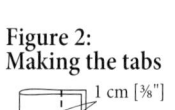

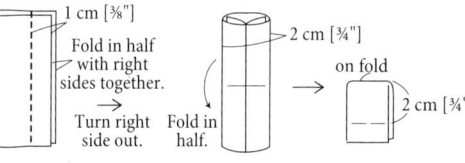

60

7 Baste handles to the pouch front and back. Matching the stars on the pouch front, pouch back, and gusset, sew right sides together. Use the bias strip to bind the seam allowances (figure 4).

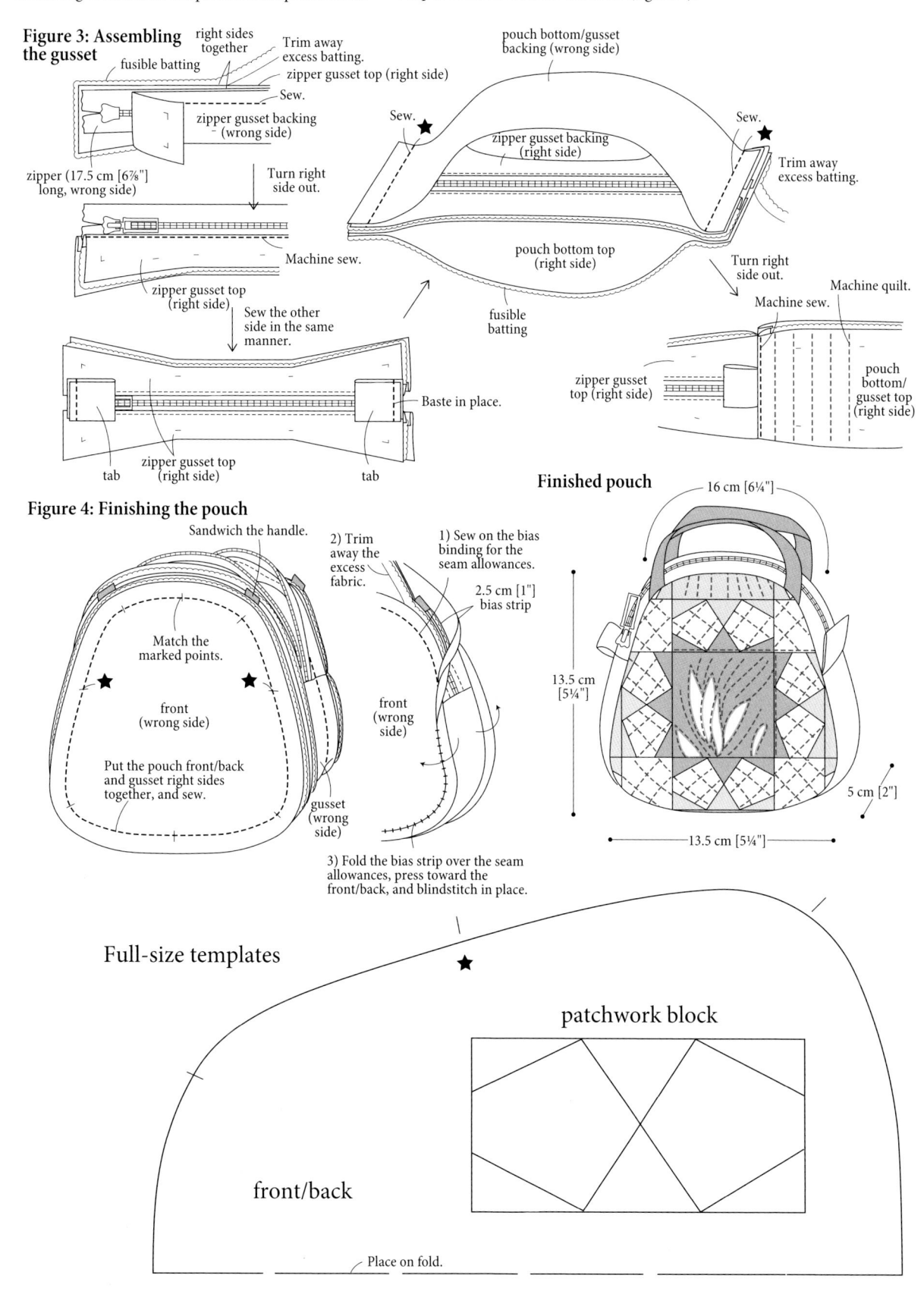

Figure 3: Assembling the gusset

Figure 4: Finishing the pouch

Finished pouch

Full-size templates

front/back

patchwork block

Place on fold.

61

05 Triangle Clasp Pouch

Project page 14 Full-size templates on page 99

Materials Needed
Cottons:
- Assorted fat quarters and scraps for patchwork
- Backing: 40 x 40 cm [16" x 16"]

Batting: 40 x 40 cm [16" x 16"]

1 pair metal purse clasps (12 x 6 cm [4¾" x 2⅜"])

Instructions
1 Sew patchwork pieces together to make two tops for the pouch and two gusset tops.
2 Put each pouch top individually with backing right sides together, then put the batting on top. Sew all around, leaving an opening to turn right side out. Turn the pouch body pieces right side out and blindstitch the opening closed. Quilt as desired (figure 1).
3 Make the two gusset pieces in the same manner as the pouch body pieces (figure 2).
4 Whipstitch and ladder stitch the pouch body and gusset together to make one continuous piece (figure 3).
5 Attach the metal clasps to the pouch body.

Pouch body: Cut 2 for top, batting, and backing.

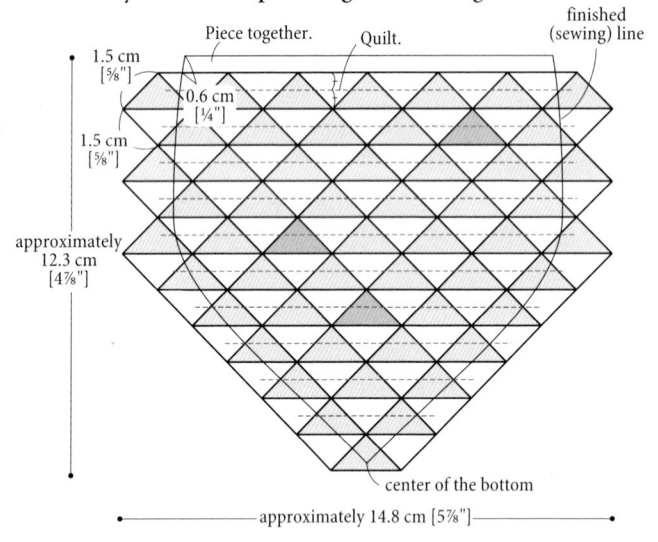

- 1.5 cm [⅝"]
- 0.6 cm [¼"]
- 1.5 cm [⅝"]
- approximately 12.3 cm [4⅞"]
- approximately 14.8 cm [5⅞"]
- Piece together. Quilt. finished (sewing) line
- center of the bottom

Gusset: Cut 2 for top, batting, and backing.

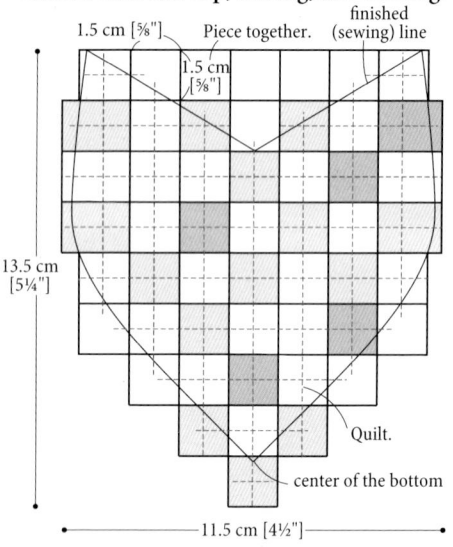

- 1.5 cm [⅝"]
- 1.5 cm [⅝"]
- 13.5 cm [5¼"]
- 11.5 cm [4½"]
- Piece together. finished (sewing) line
- Quilt. center of the bottom

- Cut all patchwork pieces with 0.7 cm [¼"] seam allowances. Cut all other pieces with 1 cm [⅜"] seam allowances.
- Piece together the half-square triangles and a strip as shown, then cut to make a pouch body top, adding 1 cm [⅜"] seam allowances. Make 2.
- Piece together the squares and rectangles as shown, then cut to make a gusset top, adding 1 cm [⅜"] seam allowances. Make 2.

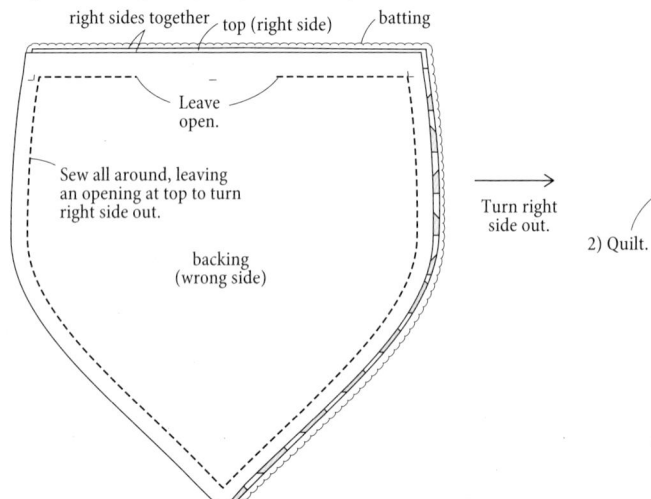

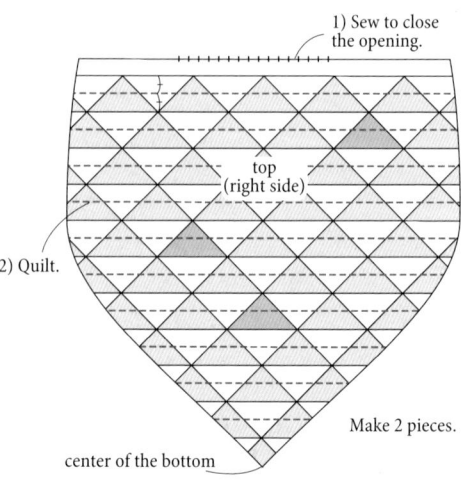

Figure 1: Preparing the pouch body

right sides together / top (right side) / batting
Leave open.
Sew all around, leaving an opening at top to turn right side out.
backing (wrong side)

→ Turn right side out.

1) Sew to close the opening.
top (right side)
2) Quilt.
Make 2 pieces.
center of the bottom

62

Figure 2: Preparing the gusset

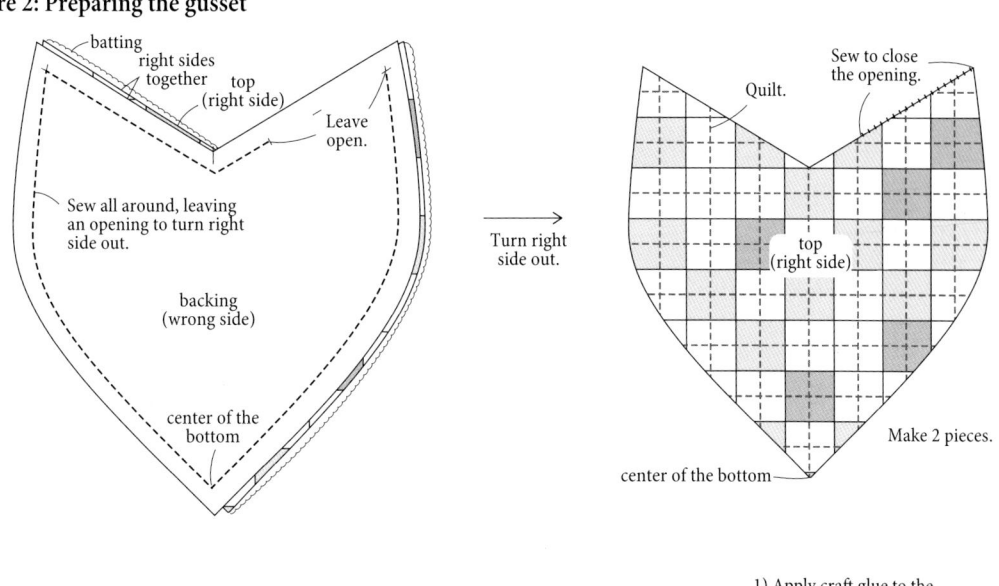

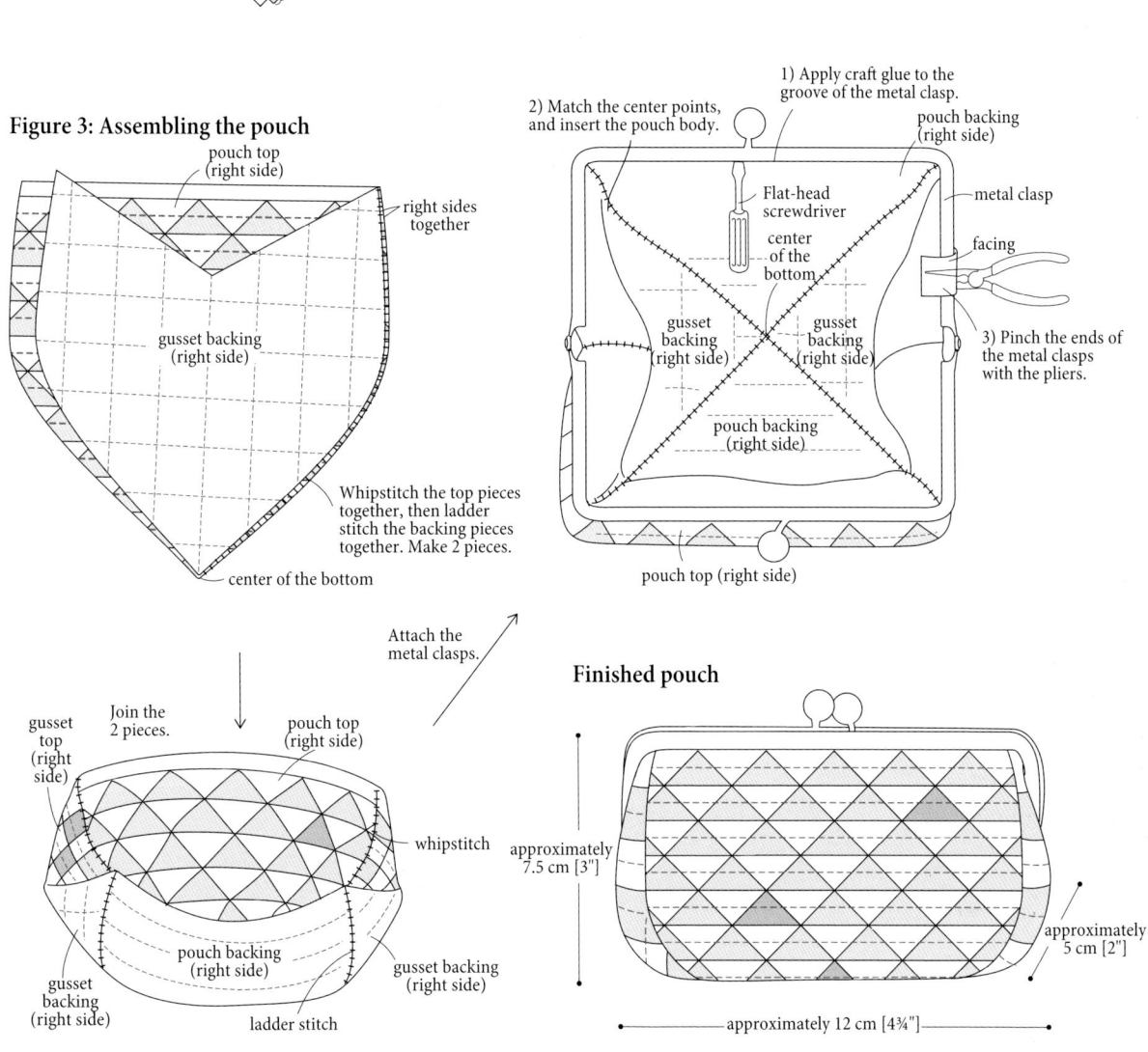

- batting
- right sides together
- top (right side)
- Leave open.
- Sew all around, leaving an opening to turn right side out.
- backing (wrong side)
- center of the bottom

Turn right side out. →

- Quilt.
- Sew to close the opening.
- top (right side)
- center of the bottom
- Make 2 pieces.

Figure 3: Assembling the pouch

- pouch top (right side)
- right sides together
- gusset backing (right side)
- Whipstitch the top pieces together, then ladder stitch the backing pieces together. Make 2 pieces.
- center of the bottom

1) Apply craft glue to the groove of the metal clasp.
2) Match the center points, and insert the pouch body.
3) Pinch the ends of the metal clasps with the pliers.

- pouch backing (right side)
- metal clasp
- Flat-head screwdriver
- facing
- center of the bottom
- gusset backing (right side)
- gusset backing (right side)
- pouch backing (right side)
- pouch top (right side)

Attach the metal clasps.

- gusset top (right side)
- Join the 2 pieces.
- pouch top (right side)
- whipstitch
- pouch backing (right side)
- gusset backing (right side)
- gusset backing (right side)
- ladder stitch

Finished pouch

- approximately 7.5 cm [3"]
- approximately 5 cm [2"]
- approximately 12 cm [4¾"]

06 Little Round Pouch

Project page 16 Full-size templates on page 65

Materials Needed

Cottons:
- Assorted fat quarters and scraps for patchwork
- Backing: 35 x 20 cm [14" x 8"]
Batting: 35 x 20 cm [14" x 8"]
12 cm [6"] zipper
1.5 cm [⅝"] wide leather tape: 10 cm [4"]

Instructions

1 Sew patchwork pieces together to make two each of pouch body A, B, and B reversed pieces and two gusset tops.
2 Put the pieces prepared in step 1 individually with backing and batting right sides together. Sew all around, leaving an opening to turn right side out.
3 Turn the pieces right side out and blindstitch the opening closed. Quilt as desired (figure 1).
4 Sew together one each of B, A, and B reversed pieces to make two pouch body halves.
5 Sew the pouch body halves and gusset together (figure 2). Shorten zipper to fit (4¾"). Sew in the zipper and tabs.

Pouch body B: Cut 2 for top, batting, and backing.
Quilt. 1 cm [⅜"]. Leave open.

Pouch body A: Cut 2 for top, batting, and backing.
1 cm [⅜"] Outline quilt. Leave open.

Pouch body B reversed: Cut 2 for top, batting, and backing.
Leave open.

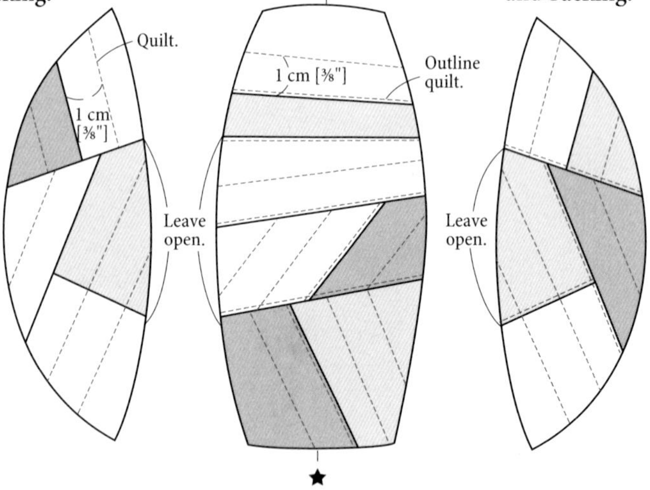

- When cutting pieces for patchwork, add 0.7 cm [¼"] seam allowances. Cut all other pieces with 1 cm [⅜"] seam allowances.
- Piece together the shapes to make pouch body A, B, and B reversed pieces. Piece together the shapes to make the gusset pieces.

Gusset: Cut 1 for top, batting, and backing.

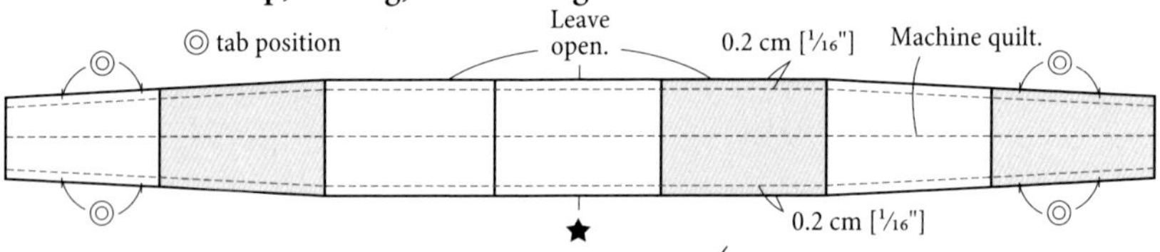

◎ tab position   Leave open.   0.2 cm [1/16"]   Machine quilt.
0.2 cm [1/16"]

Tab: Cut 2.
1.5 cm [⅝"]
leather tape (no seam allowances)
5 cm [2"]

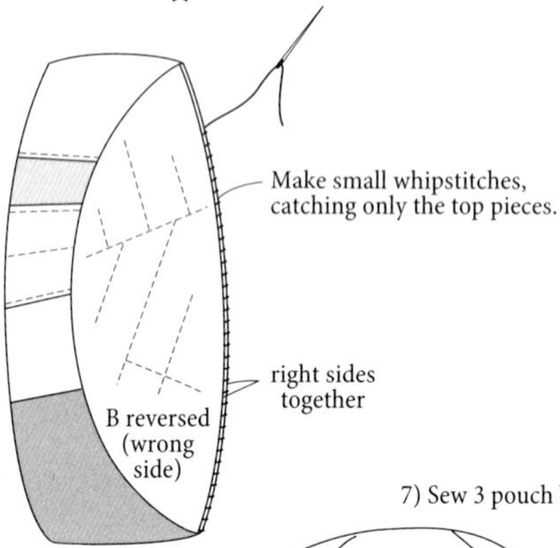

Make small whipstitches, catching only the top pieces.

right sides together
B reversed (wrong side)

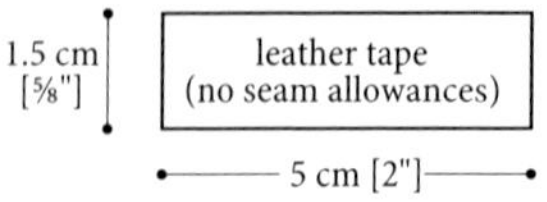

Figure 1: Assembling the pouch

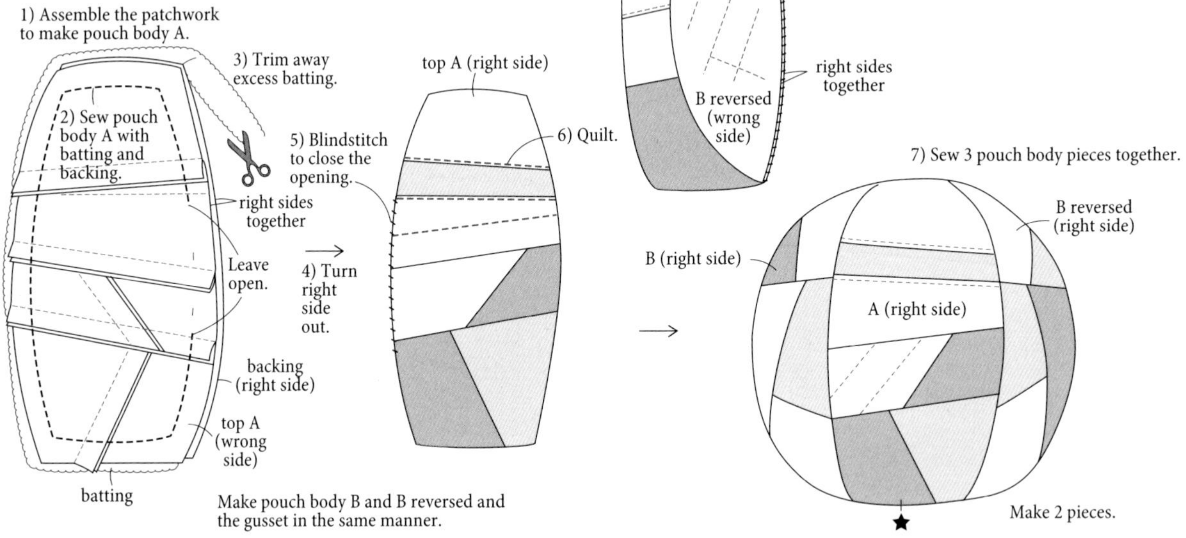

1) Assemble the patchwork to make pouch body A.
2) Sew pouch body A with batting and backing.
3) Trim away excess batting.
4) Turn right side out.
5) Blindstitch to close the opening.
6) Quilt.

right sides together
Leave open.
backing (right side)
top A (wrong side)
top A (right side)
batting

Make pouch body B and B reversed and the gusset in the same manner.

7) Sew 3 pouch body pieces together.

B reversed (right side)
B (right side)
A (right side)

Make 2 pieces.

64

Figure 2: Inserting the zipper

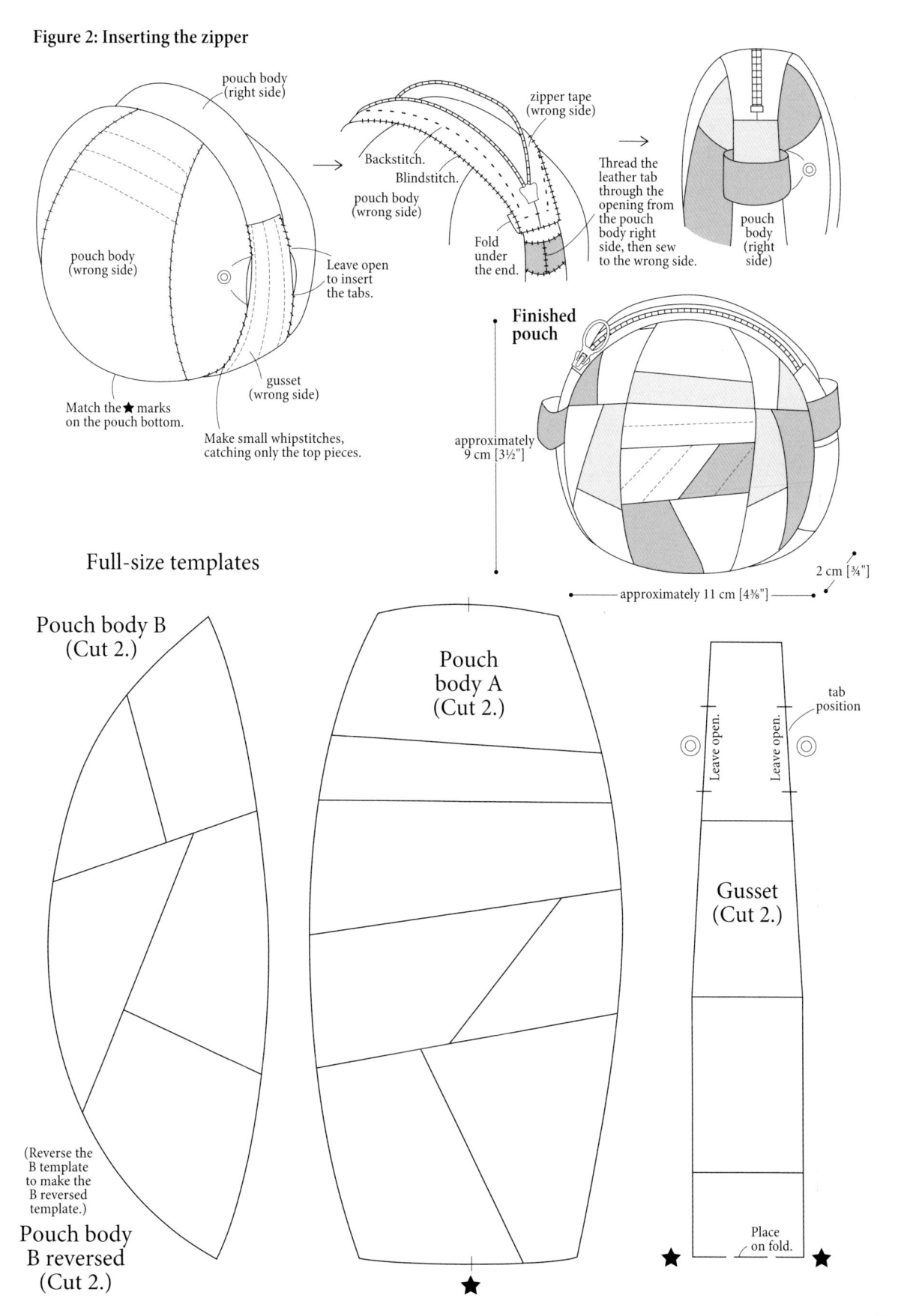

pouch body (right side)

pouch body (wrong side)

Match the ★ marks on the pouch bottom.

Leave open to insert the tabs.

gusset (wrong side)

Make small whipstitches, catching only the top pieces.

Backstitch.
Blindstitch.
pouch body (wrong side)

zipper tape (wrong side)

Fold under the end.

Thread the leather tab through the opening from the pouch body right side, then sew to the wrong side.

pouch body (right side)

Finished pouch

approximately 9 cm [3½"]

approximately 11 cm [4⅜"]

2 cm [¾"]

Full-size templates

Pouch body B (Cut 2.)

(Reverse the B template to make the B reversed template.)

Pouch body B reversed (Cut 2.)

Pouch body A (Cut 2.)

Gusset (Cut 2.)

tab position

Leave open.

Leave open.

Place on fold.

07 Tulip Pouch

Project page 18 Full-size templates on page 101

Materials Needed

Cottons:
- Background plaid for pouch body top: 25 x 25 cm [10" x 10"]
- Assorted fat quarters and scraps for appliqués
- Yarn-dyed check for gusset/pouch bottom and facing: 40 x 15 cm [16" x 6"]
- Handles: 18 x 10 cm [7" x 4"]
- Backing: 30 x 40 cm [12" x 16"]
- Bias-cut binding for seams: 2.5 x 85 cm [1" x 34"]

Batting: 30 x 40 cm [12" x 16"]
20 cm [8"] zipper; shorten to fit (7⅞")
Fusible interfacing: 3 x 25 cm [1½" x 10"]
Embroidery floss in various colors

Instructions

1 Referring to the diagram below right, stitch appliqués and embroideries on the background to make the pouch body top.
2 Layer the pouch top with batting and backing. Quilt as desired.
3 Make the handles (figure 1).

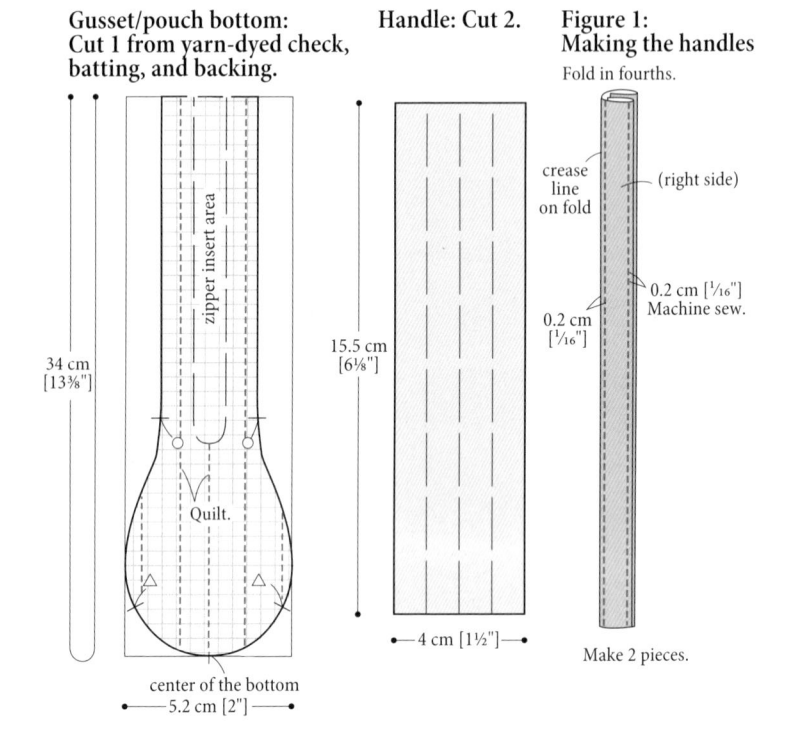

- When cutting appliqués, add 0.3 to 0.4 cm [⅛"] seam allowances. Do not add seam allowances when cutting handles. Cut all other pieces with 1 cm [⅜"] seam allowances.
- To make a facing on the gusset/pouch bottom, cut the zipper insert area from yarn-dyed check, adding 1 cm [⅜"] seam allowances. Cut the zipper insert area from interfacing, adding 0.4 cm [⅛"] seam allowances.
- Stitch appliqués and embroidery designs on the pouch body top.
- For the gusset/pouch bottom and the pouch body, make a quilt sandwich with top, batting, and backing; quilt.

Outline stitch

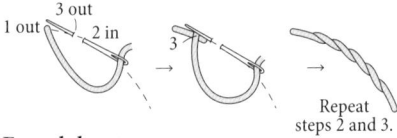

1 out, 3 out, 2 in, 3
Repeat steps 2 and 3.

French knot

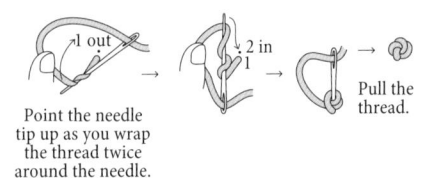

1 out, 2 in, Pull the thread.
Point the needle tip up as you wrap the thread twice around the needle.

Lazy daisy stitch

3 out, 1 out, 2 in, 4 in

Gusset/pouch bottom: Cut 1 from yarn-dyed check, batting, and backing.

zipper insert area

Quilt.

34 cm [13⅜"]

center of the bottom
5.2 cm [2"]

Handle: Cut 2.

15.5 cm [6⅛"]
4 cm [1½"]

Figure 1: Making the handles
Fold in fourths.

crease line on fold
(right side)
0.2 cm [1/16"]
0.2 cm [1/16"] Machine sew.

Make 2 pieces.

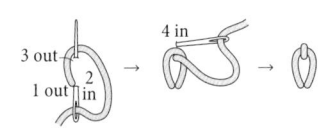

Pouch body: Cut 1 for top, batting, and backing.

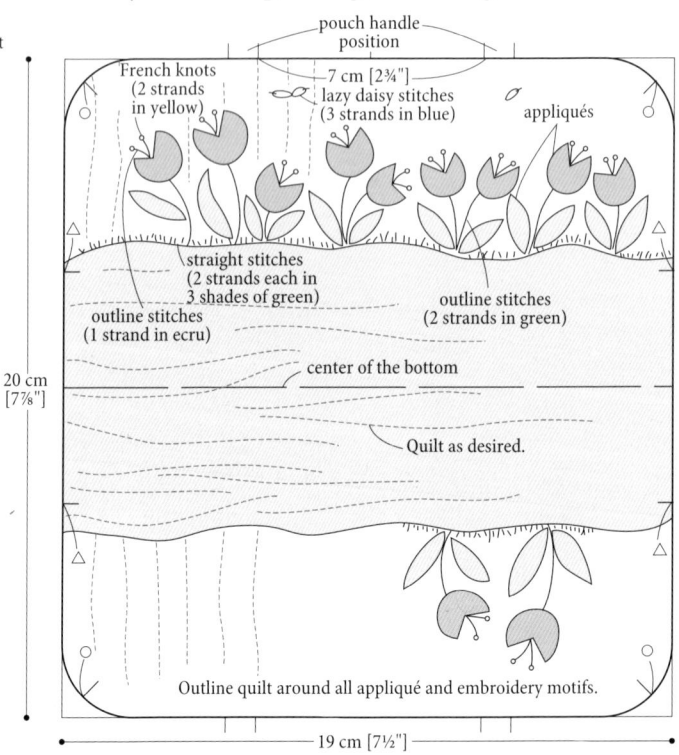

pouch handle position
7 cm [2¾"]
French knots (2 strands in yellow)
lazy daisy stitches (3 strands in blue)
appliqués
straight stitches (2 strands each in 3 shades of green)
outline stitches (1 strand in ecru)
outline stitches (2 strands in green)
center of the bottom
20 cm [7⅞"]
Quilt as desired.
Outline quilt around all appliqué and embroidery motifs.
19 cm [7½"]

4 Layer the gusset/pouch bottom top with batting and backing. Quilt as desired. Sew the facing to the right side, turn to the wrong side, and blindstitch to bind the zipper opening edges. Insert the zipper (figure 2).

5 Sew the pouch body and gusset/bottom right sides together, sandwiching the handles (figure 3).

6 Use the bias strip to bind the seam allowances in step 5.

Figure 2: Preparing the gusset/pouch bottom

yarn-dyed check facing (wrong side)
1) Center and fuse interfacing to wrong side of facing.
yarn-dyed check top (right side)
interfacing
backing (wrong side)
2) Sew.
3) Clip.
batting

facing (right side)
Bind and blindstitch.
backing (right side)
top (wrong side)
batting

zipper (wrong side)
backing (right side)
top (wrong side)
1) Sew in the zipper.
2) Whipstitch.

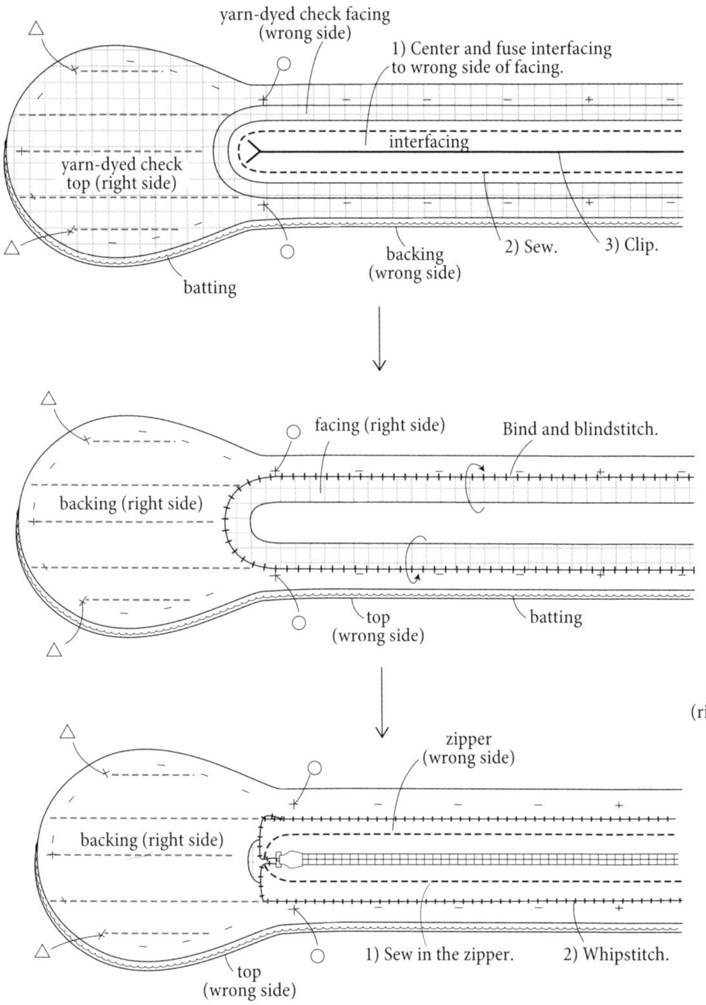

Figure 3: Assembling the pouch

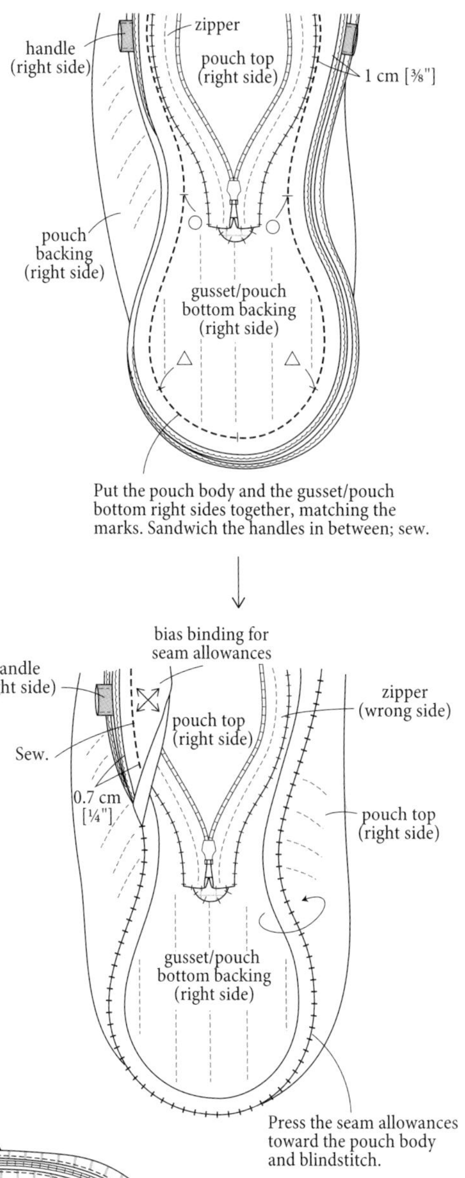

handle (right side)
zipper
pouch top (right side)
1 cm [3/8"]
pouch backing (right side)
gusset/pouch bottom backing (right side)

Put the pouch body and the gusset/pouch bottom right sides together, matching the marks. Sandwich the handles in between; sew.

bias binding for seam allowances
handle (right side)
pouch top (right side)
Sew.
0.7 cm [1/4"]
zipper (wrong side)
pouch top (right side)
gusset/pouch bottom backing (right side)

Press the seam allowances toward the pouch body and blindstitch.

Finished pouch

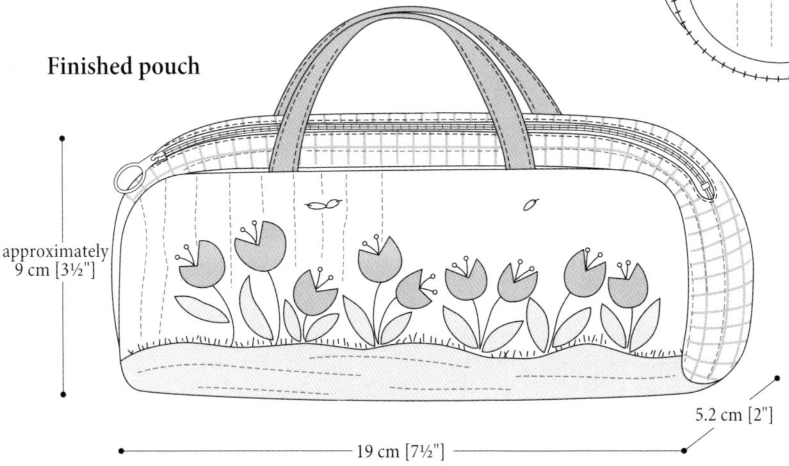

approximately 9 cm [3½"]

19 cm [7½"]

5.2 cm [2"]

67

08 See-Through Pouch

Project page 20 Full-size templates on page 69

Materials Needed for Large Pouch

Cottons:
- Assorted scraps for appliqués
- Appliqué background: 25 x 20 cm [10" x 8"]
- Backing and zipper binding: 25 x 25 cm [10" x 10"]
- Side binding: 10 x 20 cm [4" x 8"]

Front vinyl: 12.5 x 21 cm [4⅞" x 8¼"]
21 cm [9"] separating zipper
Decorative zipper pull
Double-sided fusible web: 15 x 22 cm [6" x 9"]

Materials Needed for Small Pouch

Cottons:
- Assorted scraps for appliqués
- Appliqué background: 20 x 20 cm [8" x 8"]
- Backing and zipper binding: 25 x 20 cm [10" x 8"]
- Side binding: 10 x 15 cm [4" x 6"]

Front vinyl: 10 x 17 cm [3⅞" x 6⅝"]
17 cm [7"] separating zipper
Double-sided fusible web: 10 x 22 cm [4" x 9"]

Large pouch back: Cut 1 each for appliqué background and backing.

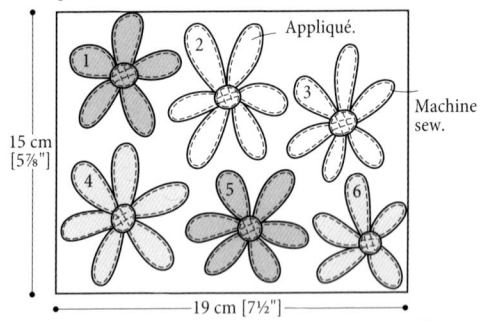

15 cm [5⅞"] × 19 cm [7½"]

Appliqué. Machine sew.

Do not add seam allowances when cutting appliqués. Add 1 cm [⅜"] seam allowances to all edges of pouch back and to side and bottom edges of pouch front.

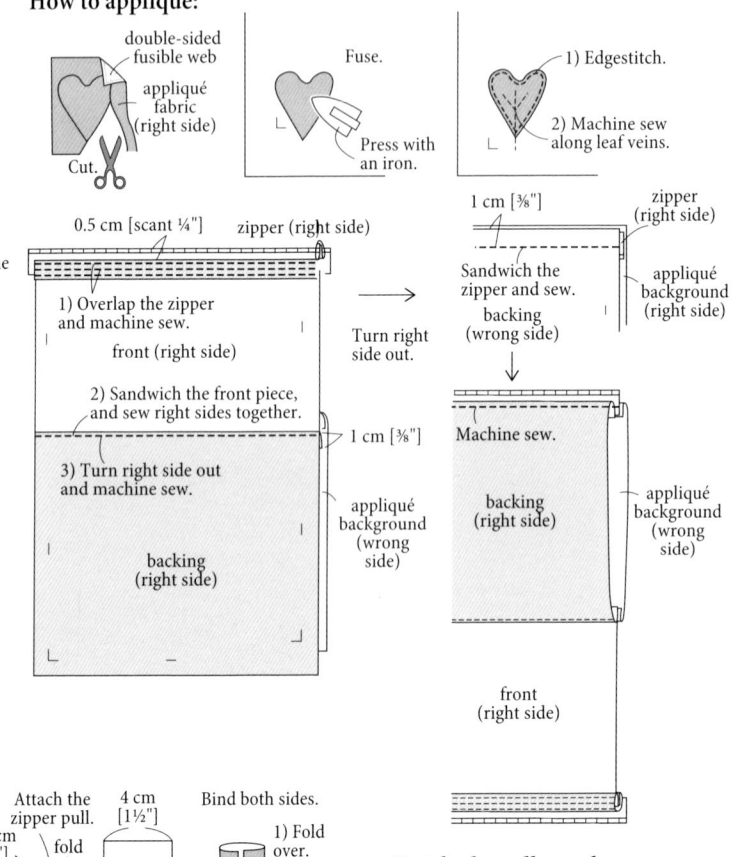

Large pouch front: Cut 1 from vinyl.

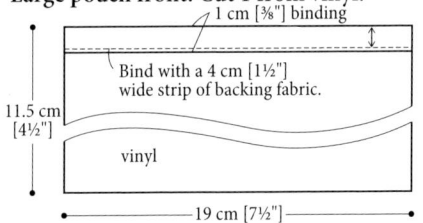

1 cm [⅜"] binding
Bind with a 4 cm [1½"] wide strip of backing fabric.
vinyl
11.5 cm [4½"] × 19 cm [7½"]

Small pouch back: Cut 1 each for appliqué background and backing.

13 cm [5⅛"] × 15 cm [5⅞"]

Appliqué. Machine sew.

Do not add seam allowances when cutting appliqués. Add 1 cm [⅜"] seam allowances to all edges of pouch back and to side and bottom edges of pouch front.

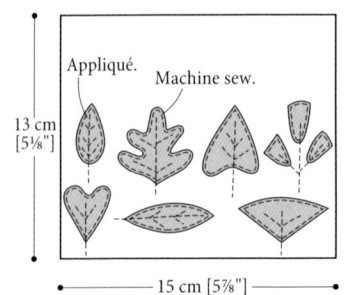

Small pouch front: Cut 1 from vinyl.

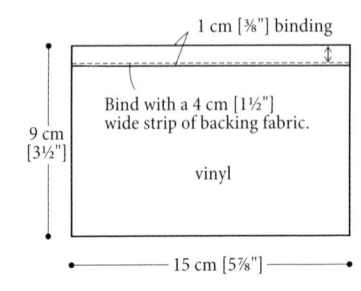

1 cm [⅜"] binding
Bind with a 4 cm [1½"] wide strip of backing fabric.
vinyl
9 cm [3½"] × 15 cm [5⅞"]

How to appliqué:

double-sided fusible web
appliqué fabric (right side)
Cut.

Fuse. Press with an iron.

1) Edgestitch.
2) Machine sew along leaf veins.

0.5 cm [scant ¼"] zipper (right side)
1) Overlap the zipper and machine sew.
front (right side)
2) Sandwich the front piece, and sew right sides together.
3) Turn right side out and machine sew.
backing (right side)
appliqué background (wrong side)
1 cm [⅜"]

Turn right side out.

1 cm [⅜"] zipper (right side)
Sandwich the zipper and sew.
appliqué background (right side)
backing (wrong side)

Machine sew.
backing (right side)
appliqué background (wrong side)
front (right side)

Attach the zipper pull.
1.5 cm [⅝"] fold
1 cm [⅜"]
4 cm [1½"]
9 cm [3½"] front (wrong side)

Bind both sides.
1) Fold over.
1 cm [⅜"]
2) Fold to backing.
backing (right side)
1 cm [⅜"]
Blindstitch.

Finished large pouch

1 cm [⅜"] back (right side)
11.5 cm [4½"]
14 cm [5½"]
21 cm [8¼"]

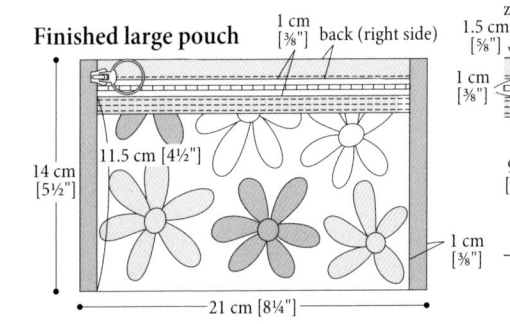

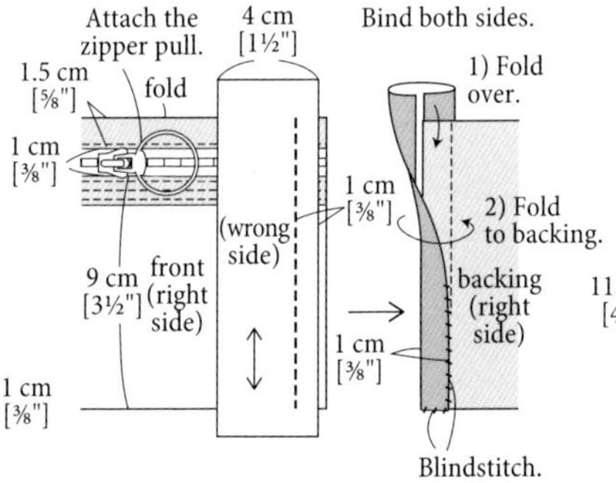

Finished small pouch

11.5 cm [4½"]
17 cm [6"]

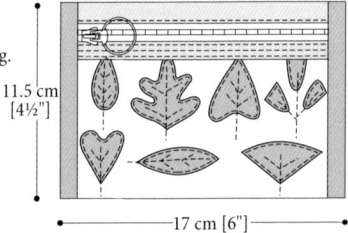

Instructions
1 Stitch appliqués on the appliqué background.
2 Bind the top edge of the vinyl front and topstitch the binding over the bottom edge of the zipper.
3 Sandwich the bottom edge of the vinyl front between the appliqué background and backing rectangles. Sew through all layers. Open the rectangles, finger-press, and topstitch. Separate the zipper and sandwich the remaining zipper tape between the appliqué background and backing rectangles; sew.

4 Attach the pull to the zipper. Fold the pouch in half with wrong sides together. Bind each side with binding strips.

Appliqué motifs

69

09 Drawstring Pouch

Project page 21
Full-size templates on page 71

Materials Needed

Cottons:
- Gray print for pouch front and back: 50 x 25 cm [20" x 10"]
- Assorted fat quarters and scraps for appliqués and decorations for the string tips
- Lining: 50 x 25 cm [20" x 10"]

Cord or string (0.2 cm [1/16"] in diameter): 110 cm [44"]

Embroidery floss in brown

Pouch front/back: Cut 2 each from top fabric and lining.

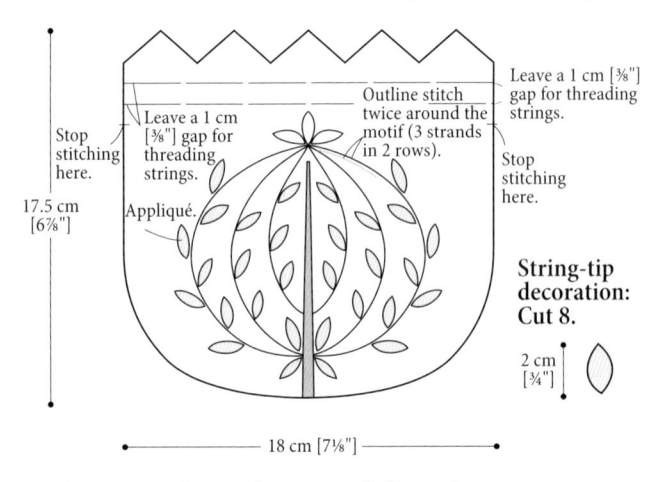

- Leave a 1 cm [3/8"] gap for threading strings.
- Stop stitching here.
- Outline stitch twice around the motif (3 strands in 2 rows).
- Stop stitching here.
- Appliqué.
- 17.5 cm [6⅞"]
- 18 cm [7⅛"]

String-tip decoration: Cut 8.
- 2 cm [¾"]

- When cutting appliqués, add 0.3 to 0.4 cm [⅛"] seam allowances. Cut string-tip decoration pieces with 0.7 cm [¼"] seam allowances. Cut all other pieces with 1 cm [⅜"] seam allowances.
- Stitch appliqués and embroidery designs on the pouch front.

Figure 1: Preparing the pouch front

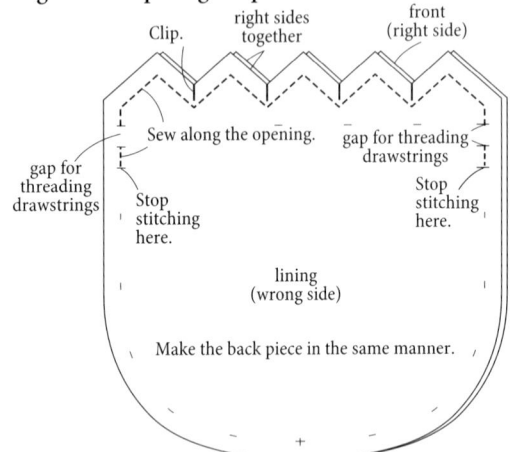

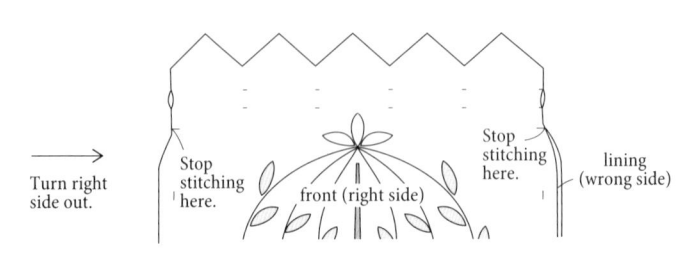

- Clip.
- right sides together
- front (right side)
- Sew along the opening.
- gap for threading drawstrings
- Stop stitching here.
- gap for threading drawstrings
- Stop stitching here.
- lining (wrong side)
- Make the back piece in the same manner.

Turn right side out.

- Stop stitching here.
- front (right side)
- Stop stitching here.
- lining (wrong side)

Make the pouch back piece in the same manner.

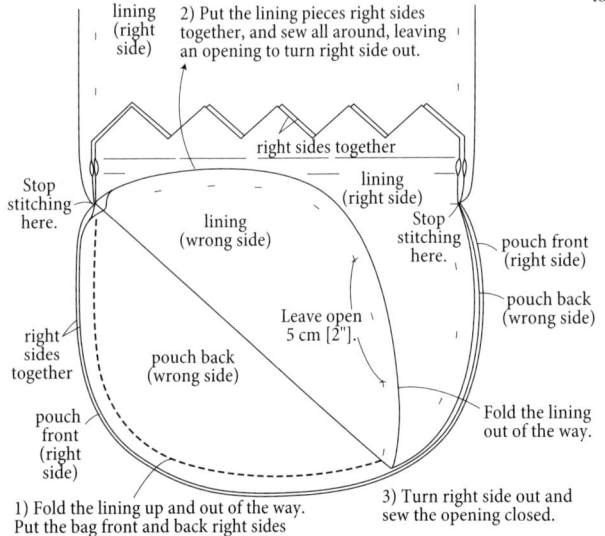

Figure 3: Assembling the string-tip decoration

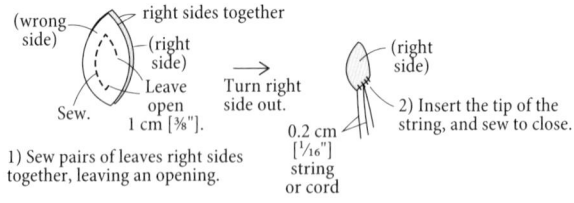

- (wrong side)
- (right side)
- right sides together
- Sew.
- Leave open 1 cm [⅜"].
- Turn right side out.
- (right side)
- 0.2 cm [1/16"] string or cord
- 2) Insert the tip of the string, and sew to close.

1) Sew pairs of leaves right sides together, leaving an opening.

Figure 2: Assembling the pouch

- lining (right side)
- 2) Put the lining pieces right sides together, and sew all around, leaving an opening to turn right side out.
- right sides together
- Stop stitching here.
- lining (right side)
- lining (wrong side)
- Stop stitching here.
- pouch front (right side)
- pouch back (wrong side)
- Leave open 5 cm [2"].
- right sides together
- pouch back (wrong side)
- pouch front (right side)
- Fold the lining out of the way.

1) Fold the lining up and out of the way. Put the bag front and back right sides together, and sew between the marks.

3) Turn right side out and sew the opening closed.

Finished pouch

Thread one length of string or cord through one opening, all the way around and out the same opening you went in. Repeat from the other side with the second length of string or cord.

- Machine sew a 1 cm [⅜"] wide gap.
- 17.5 cm [6⅞"]
- 18 cm [7⅛"]
- 55 cm [21⅝"] length of 0.2 cm [1/16"] string or cord

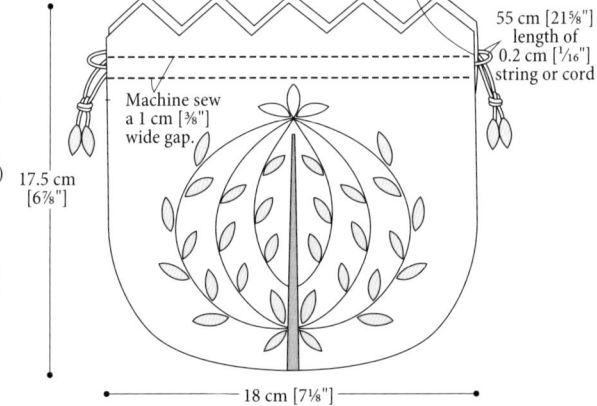

Instructions

1 Referring to the diagram on page 70 and the pattern below, stitch appliqués and embroideries on the background to make the pouch front top.

2 Put the piece prepared in step 1 and lining together. Sew all around between marks, leaving open a gap at the top for threading strings (figure 1). Make the pouch back in the same manner.

3 Sew the pouch front and back along the bag bottom. Then sew the front and back lining together along the bag bottom, leaving a 5 cm [2"] opening to turn right side out (figure 2).

4 Turn the piece right side out and sew the opening closed.

5 Sew a channel on the pouch front and then on the pouch back. Thread two strings through the channel as shown in Finished pouch diagram on page 70.

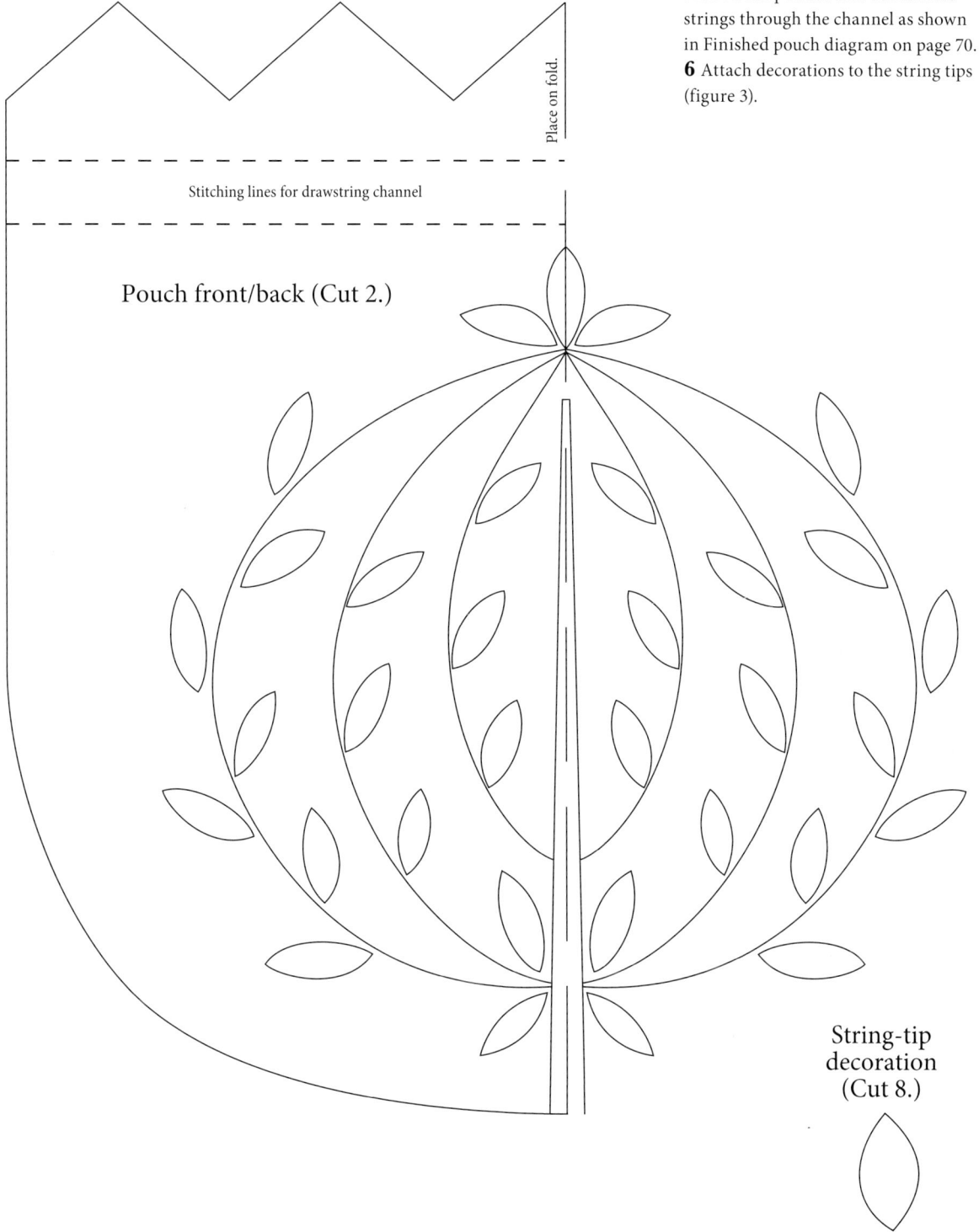

6 Attach decorations to the string tips (figure 3).

Full-size templates

Place on fold.

Stitching lines for drawstring channel

Pouch front/back (Cut 2.)

String-tip decoration (Cut 8.)

10 Tiny Tote

Project page 22   Templates on page 73

Materials Needed

Cottons:
- Yarn-dyed plaid for tote body top: 45 x 10 cm [18" x 4"]
- Assorted fat quarters and scraps for appliqués
- Green print for tote bottom and patchwork: 20 x 15 cm [8" x 6"]
- Brown print for handles: 10 x 25 cm [4" x 10"]
- Bias binding: 3.5 x 45 cm [1⅜" x 18"]
- Lining and facing fabric: 45 x 25 cm [18" x 10"] each

Batting and heavyweight fusible interfacing: 45 x 25 cm [18" x 10"] each

Lightweight fusible interfacing: 10 x 20 cm [4" x 8"]
4 buttons (1 cm [⅜"] in diameter)
Double-sided fusible web
Thread in gold

Instructions

1 Center and fuse lightweight interfacing to wrong side of handle pieces and make handles (figure 1).
2 Referring to the diagrams below and the templates on page 73, stitch appliqués and embroideries on the tote body top fabric. Layer with batting and facing; quilt. Sew the ends of the quilted tote body together (figure 2).
3 Layer the tote bottom with batting and facing; machine quilt (figure 3).
4 Sew the tote body and bottom together. Blindstitch the seam allowances to the bottom (figure 4).
5 Center and fuse the heavyweight interfacing to the lining body and lining bottom. Sew together (figure 5).
6 Insert the lining into the tote body and bind the opening edges (figure 6).
7 Secure the handles to the tote opening with buttons.

Tote body: Cut 1 each from top fabric, batting, facing, lining, and heavyweight interfacing.

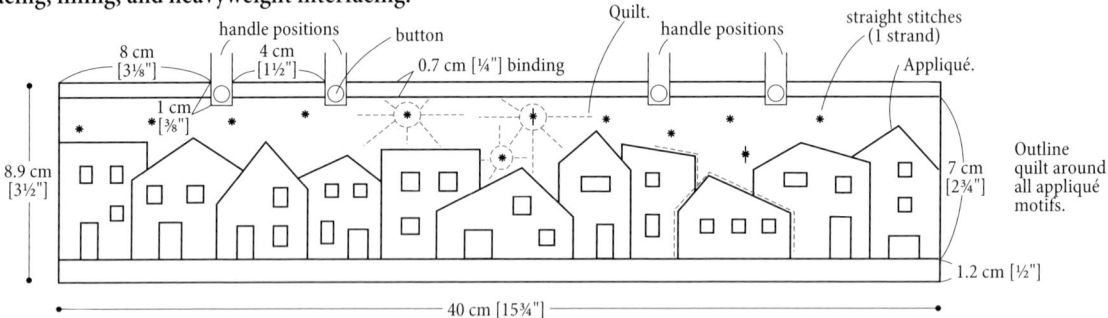

- 8 cm [3⅛"]
- handle positions
- 4 cm [1½"]
- button
- 1 cm [⅜"]
- 0.7 cm [¼"] binding
- Quilt.
- handle positions
- straight stitches (1 strand)
- Appliqué.
- 8.9 cm [3½"]
- 7 cm [2¾"]
- Outline quilt around all appliqué motifs.
- 1.2 cm [½"]
- 40 cm [15¾"]

Tote bottom: Cut 1 each from top fabric, batting, facing, lining, and heavyweight interfacing.

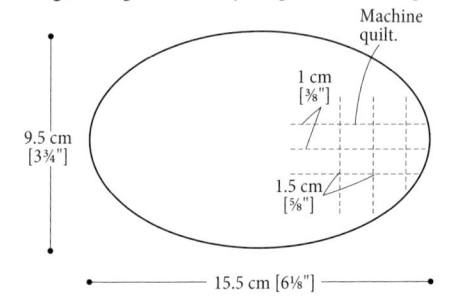

- Machine quilt.
- 1 cm [⅜"]
- 1.5 cm [⅝"]
- 9.5 cm [3¾"]
- 15.5 cm [6⅛"]

- Do not add seam allowances when cutting interfacing. When cutting appliqués, add 0.3 to 0.4 cm [⅛"] seam allowances. Cut all other pieces with 0.7 cm [¼"] seam allowances.
- Stitch appliqués and embroidery designs on the tote body top, then sew the green print strip to the bottom edge.

Handle: Cut 2 each from brown print and lightweight interfacing.

- Center and fuse lightweight interfacing to the handle wrong side.
- 0.5 cm [scant ¼"]
- 0.5 cm [scant ¼"]
- 4.5 cm [1¾"]
- no seam allowances
- 20.5 cm [8"]

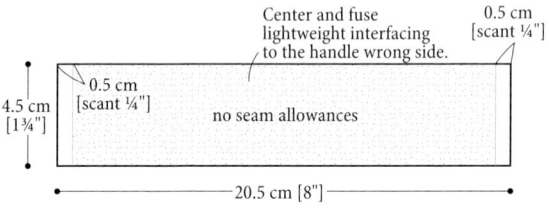

Figure 1: Making the handles

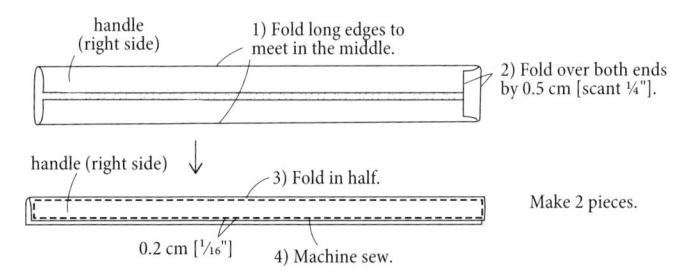

- handle (right side)
- 1) Fold long edges to meet in the middle.
- 2) Fold over both ends by 0.5 cm [scant ¼"].
- handle (right side)
- 3) Fold in half.
- 0.2 cm [1/16"]
- 4) Machine sew.
- Make 2 pieces.

Figure 2: Preparing the tote body

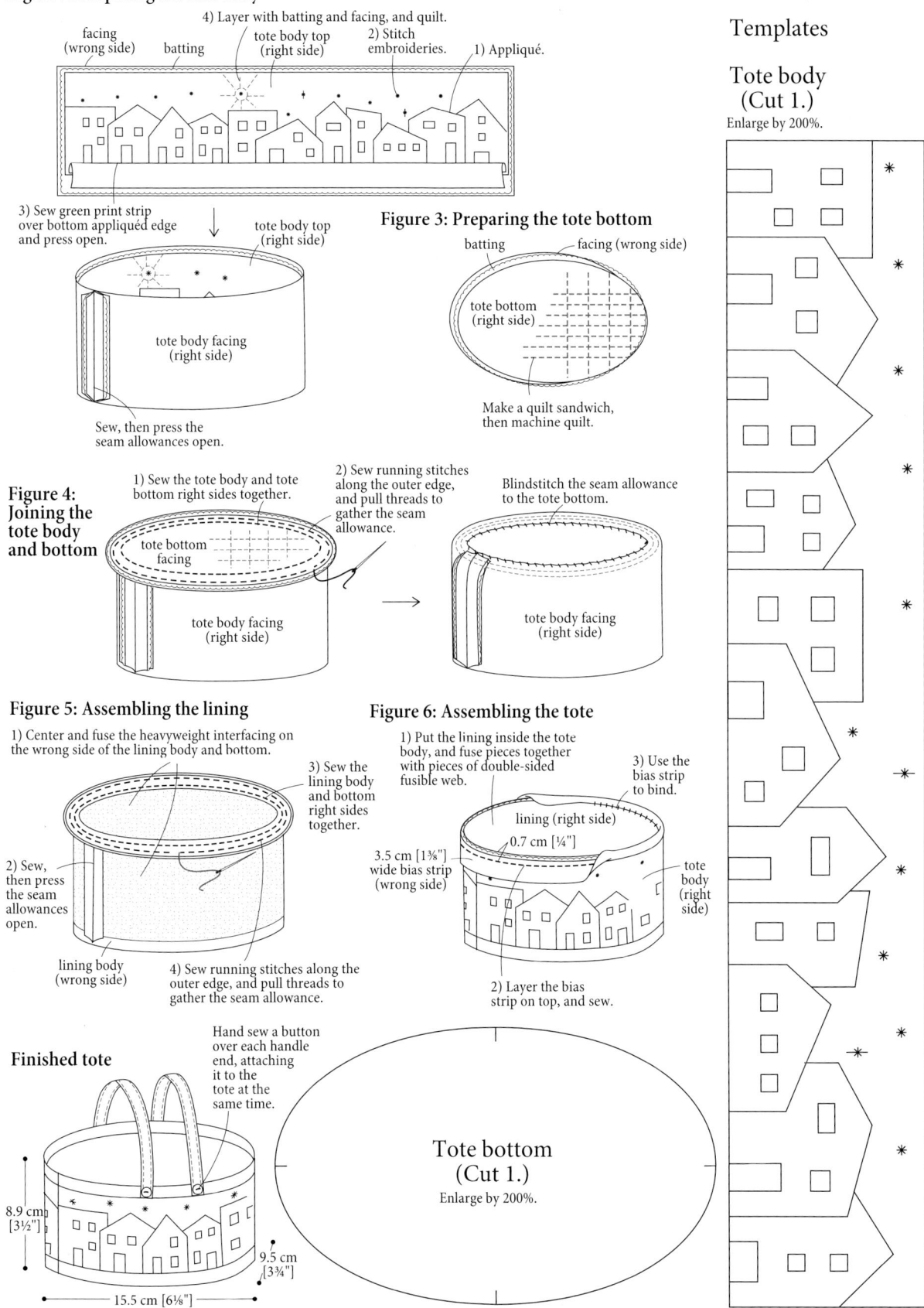

- 1) Appliqué.
- 2) Stitch embroideries.
- 3) Sew green print strip over bottom appliquéd edge and press open.
- 4) Layer with batting and facing, and quilt.

facing (wrong side)
batting
tote body top (right side)

tote body top (right side)
tote body facing (right side)
Sew, then press the seam allowances open.

Figure 3: Preparing the tote bottom

batting
facing (wrong side)
tote bottom (right side)

Make a quilt sandwich, then machine quilt.

Figure 4: Joining the tote body and bottom

1) Sew the tote body and tote bottom right sides together.
2) Sew running stitches along the outer edge, and pull threads to gather the seam allowance.

tote bottom facing
tote body facing (right side)

Blindstitch the seam allowance to the tote bottom.

tote body facing (right side)

Figure 5: Assembling the lining

1) Center and fuse the heavyweight interfacing on the wrong side of the lining body and bottom.
2) Sew, then press the seam allowances open.
3) Sew the lining body and bottom right sides together.
4) Sew running stitches along the outer edge, and pull threads to gather the seam allowance.

lining body (wrong side)

Figure 6: Assembling the tote

1) Put the lining inside the tote body, and fuse pieces together with pieces of double-sided fusible web.
2) Layer the bias strip on top, and sew.
3) Use the bias strip to bind.

lining (right side)
0.7 cm [¼"]
3.5 cm [1⅜"] wide bias strip (wrong side)
tote body (right side)

Finished tote

Hand sew a button over each handle end, attaching it to the tote at the same time.

8.9 cm [3½"]
9.5 cm [3¾"]
15.5 cm [6⅛"]

Templates

Tote body (Cut 1.)
Enlarge by 200%.

Tote bottom (Cut 1.)
Enlarge by 200%.

73

11, 12
Bunny Dolls

Project page 24 Full-size templates on page 102

Materials Needed for 1 Bunny
Cottons
- Fabric A yarn-dye: 12 x 6 cm [2⅜" x 4¾"]
- Fabric B print: 30 x 8 cm [11¾" x 3⅛"]
- Fabric C: 30 x 8 cm [11¾" x 3⅛"]
- Tweed: 40 x 10 cm [16" x 4"]

Fusible batting: 10 x 10 cm [4" x 4"]
Embroidery floss in various colors
Cotton stuffing

(Only for the boy bunny)
0.5 cm [scant ¼"] wide tape: 20 cm [8"]
4 buttons (0.7 cm [¼"] in diameter)

Instructions
1 Refer to the cutting diagrams and figures 1–3 to cut fabric and make legs, arms, and ears individually.
2 Assemble the head and torso; stuff (figure 4).
3 Sew the legs, arms, and ears to the torso (figure 5).
4 Attach suspenders on the boy bunny.
5 Embroider facial features.

Cutting layout

Fabric A (same for both bunnies) — inner ear, Place on fold. 6 cm [2⅜"] × 12 cm [4¾"]

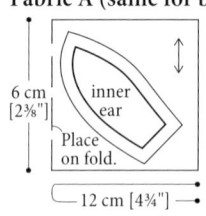

Fabric B (same for both bunnies) — Place on fold. torso, arm, arm. 8 cm [3⅛"] × 30 cm [11¾"]

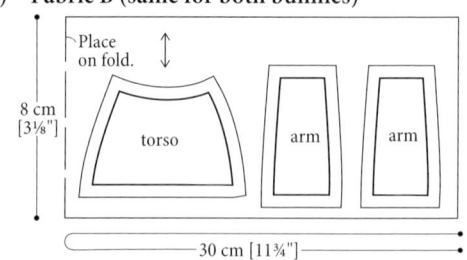

Tweed (same for both bunnies) — Place on fold. outer ear, head, head, leg, leg, paw, paw. 10 cm [4"] × 40 cm [15¾"]

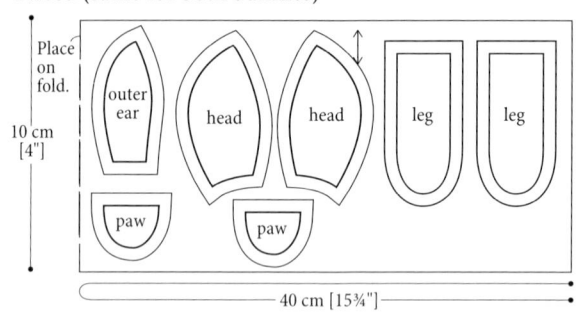

When cutting, add 0.5 cm [scant ¼"] seam allowances to all pieces. Also cut the outer ears from fusible batting.

Fabric C (for the boy bunny) — pants, pant leg, pant leg. Place on fold. 8 cm [3⅛"] × 30 cm [11¾"]

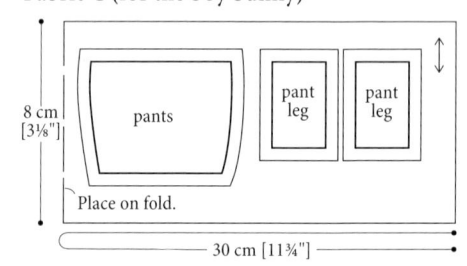

Fabric C (for the girl bunny) — skirt. Place on fold. 8 cm [3⅛"] × 20 cm [7⅞"]

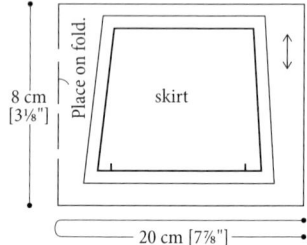

Figure 1: Assembling the legs

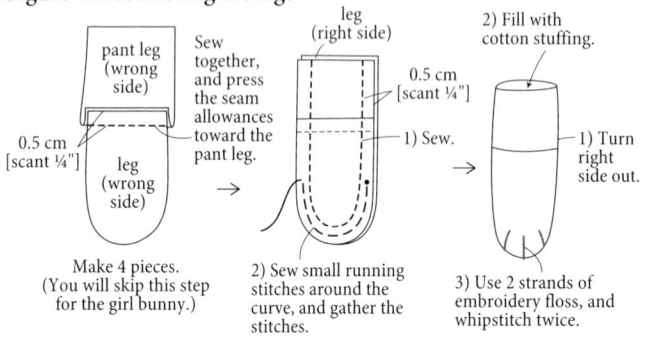

pant leg (wrong side) — Sew together, and press the seam allowances toward the pant leg. 0.5 cm [scant ¼"] leg (wrong side)

Make 4 pieces. (You will skip this step for the girl bunny.)

2) Sew small running stitches around the curve, and gather the stitches.

leg (right side) — 1) Sew. 0.5 cm [scant ¼"]

2) Fill with cotton stuffing.
1) Turn right side out.
3) Use 2 strands of embroidery floss, and whipstitch twice.

Figure 2: Assembling the paws and arms

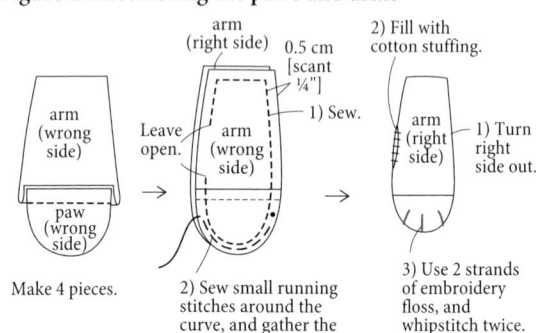

arm (right side), arm (wrong side), Leave open., paw (wrong side) — 1) Sew. 0.5 cm [scant ¼"]

Make 4 pieces.

2) Sew small running stitches around the curve, and gather the stitches.

arm (right side) — 1) Turn right side out.

2) Fill with cotton stuffing.
3) Use 2 strands of embroidery floss, and whipstitch twice.

Figure 3: Assembling the ears

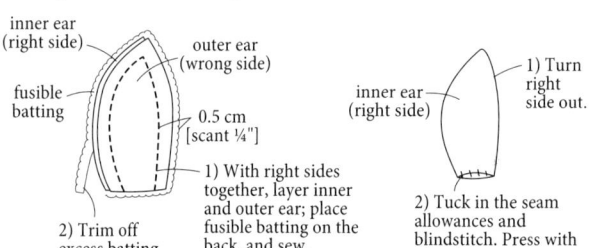

inner ear (right side), outer ear (wrong side), fusible batting — 0.5 cm [scant ¼"]

1) With right sides together, layer inner and outer ear; place fusible batting on the back, and sew.
2) Trim off excess batting.

inner ear (right side) — 1) Turn right side out.
2) Tuck in the seam allowances and blindstitch. Press with a hot iron to fuse.

Make 1 piece each for the left and right sides.

Figure 4: Assembling the head and torso

- head (right side)
- 0.5 cm [scant ¼"]
- head (wrong side)
- Sew to the marked point.
- 2) Sew together and press the seam allowances downward.
- Press the seam allowances open.
- head (wrong side)
- 1) Sew to the marked point.
- torso (wrong side)
- 0.5 cm [scant ¼"]
- pants (wrong side/boy)
- skirt (wrong side/girl)
- Make 2 pieces.
- 2) Sew small running stitches around the curve and gather the stitches.
- 0.3 cm [⅛"]
- head (wrong side)
- 0.5 cm [scant ¼"]
- head (right side)
- torso (wrong side)
- 1) Sew the head/torso pieces together.
- Leave open.
- 1) Turn right side out.
- 2) Fill with cotton stuffing.
- 3) Tuck in the seam allowances.

Figure 5: Assembling the bunny

- 2 cm [¾"]
- outer ear (right side)
- 2) Fold in half.
- 3) Stitch to the seam.
- 0.7 cm [¼"]
- 4) Sew.
- 1) Sandwich the legs, and sew to close.
- Make the girl bunny in the same manner as the boy bunny except for the suspenders.
- 10 cm [4"] of tape
- 2) Cross over.
- 2.3 cm [⅞"]
- 1) Sew to secure with a button.
- 3) Embroider the facial features.
- 23 cm [9"]
- 2) Trim off excess tape.
- 2 cm [¾"]
- 1) Secure in place with a button.

Finished bunnies

Padded satin stitch

1 out, 3 out, c in, 2 in, b out, a in

Repeat steps 2 and 3.

Stitch one or more lines of running stitches (a, b, c) within the motif. Then cover the motif with satin stitches. When deciding on the direction of your stitching, know that it is easier to start stitching from the widest portion of the motif.

When you reach the tip of the motif, bury your needle in the satin stitches on the wrong side. Come up just on the other half of where you started satin stitching and complete the other half.

Embroidered facial features

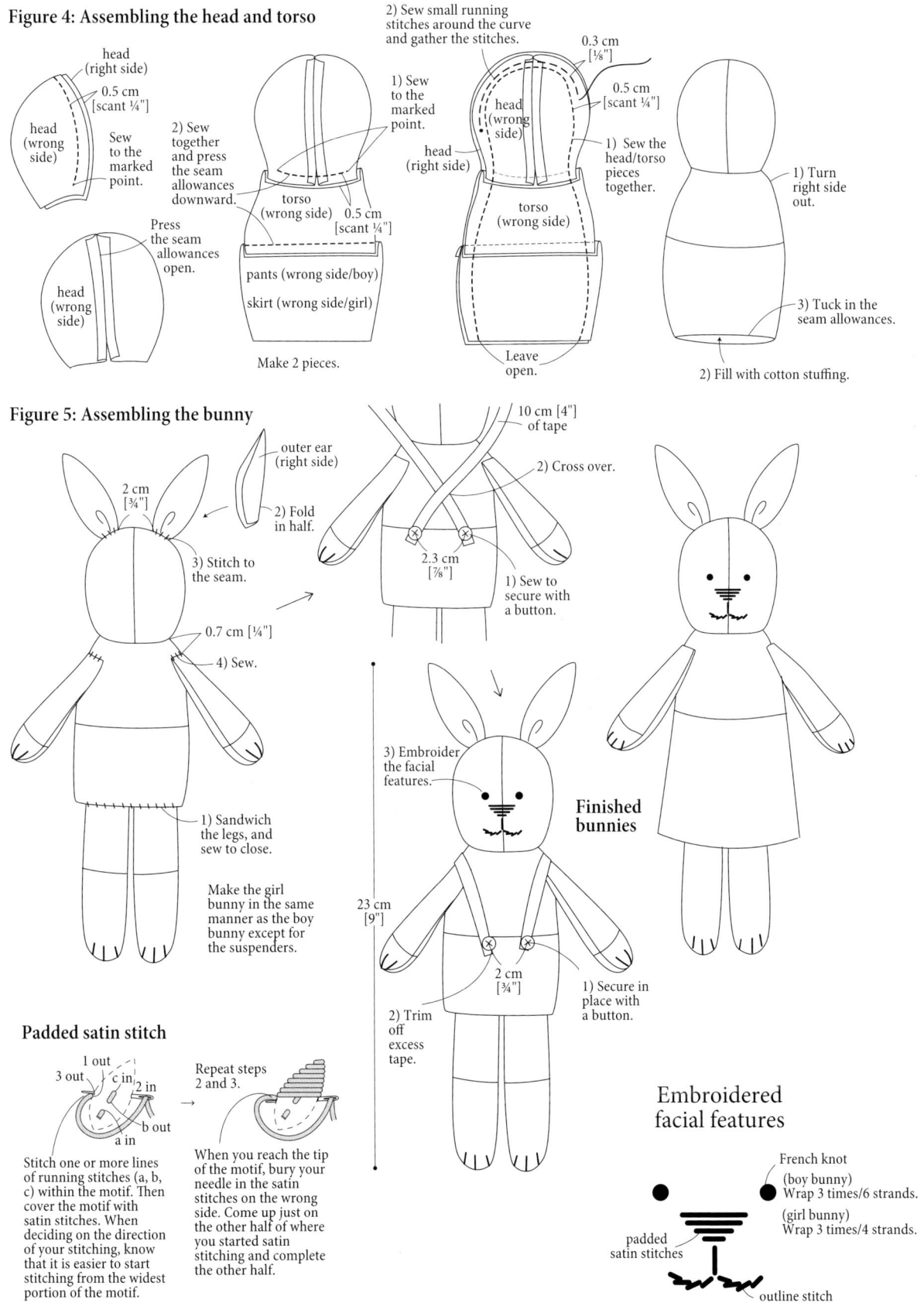

- French knot
  - (boy bunny) Wrap 3 times/6 strands.
  - (girl bunny) Wrap 3 times/4 strands.
- padded satin stitches
- outline stitch

Use 2 strands of embroidery floss for satin and outline stitch.

13, 14
Miniature Boxes

Project page 26 Templates on page 78

Materials Needed for 1 Box
Same for project 13 or 14.
Cottons:
- Assorted fat quarters and scraps for box body, appliqués, and tabs
- Lining and facing: 35 x 30 cm [14" x 12"] each

Batting: 35 x 30 cm [14" x 12"]
Plastic board or template plastic: 30 x 20 cm [12" x 8"]
Embroidery floss in various colors

For Project 13 only:
1 decorative button (1.1 cm [½"] diameter)
1 button for reinforcement on inside of box
Cord (0.3 cm [⅛"] in diameter): 6 cm [2⅜"]
No. 5 perle cotton in beige

For Project 14 only:
Magnetic closure (1.1 cm [½"] diameter): 1 pair

Instructions
1 Referring to the diagrams at right and the templates on page 78, stitch appliqués and embroideries on the patchwork piece for each wall, bottom, and roof.
2 For Project 13, assemble the chicken coop roof as shown (figure 1).
3 Piece patches to make the box body; layer with batting and facing. Quilt as desired (figure 2).
4 Put the lining on the piece prepared in step 3. Sew along both sides and turn right side out (figure 3). Put the plastic boards between the box body and lining; stitch in the ditch between the plastic boards after inserting each one.
5 Sandwich a loop (Project 13) or a tab (Project 14) in the opening and hand sew to close the opening.
6 Ladder stitch to sew the walls together.
7 Sew the button on for Project 13.

Chicken coop: Cut 1 for top, plastic board, batting, facing, and lining.

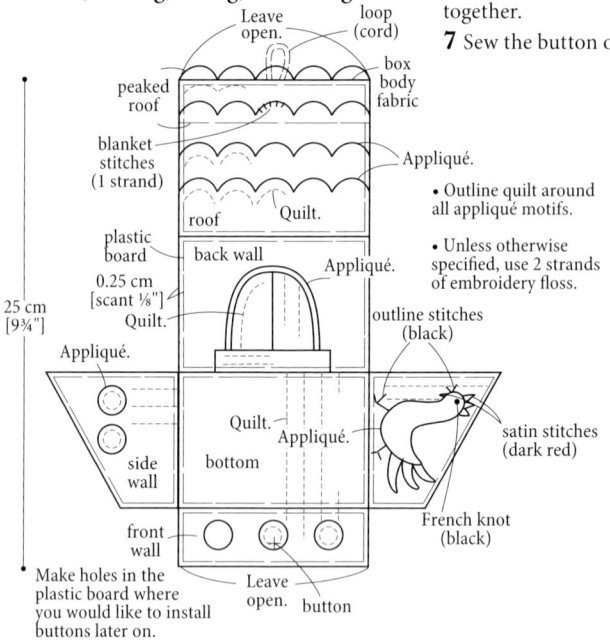

- Leave open.
- loop (cord)
- peaked roof
- box body fabric
- blanket stitches (1 strand)
- Appliqué.
- roof — Quilt.
- plastic board 0.25 cm [scant ⅛"]
- back wall
- Appliqué.
- 25 cm [9¾"]
- Quilt.
- Appliqué.
- side wall
- Quilt.
- Appliqué.
- bottom
- outline stitches (black)
- satin stitches (dark red)
- French knot (black)
- front wall
- Leave open.
- button
- Make holes in the plastic board where you would like to install buttons later on.
- 7 cm [2¾"] — 10 cm [4"] — 7 cm [2¾"]

- Outline quilt around all appliqué motifs.
- Unless otherwise specified, use 2 strands of embroidery floss.

Doghouse: Cut 1 for top, plastic board, batting, facing, and lining.

- tab position
- Leave open.
- plastic board
- roof — Quilt.
- 0.25 cm [scant ⅛"]
- wall
- Appliqué.
- 26.2 cm [10¼"]
- Appliqué.
- side wall
- bottom
- outline stitches (5 strands in brown)
- straight stitches (black)
- Bullion stitch (black)
- French knot (3 strands in black)
- Leave open.
- tab position
- 10 cm [4"] — 10 cm [4"] — 10 cm [4"]

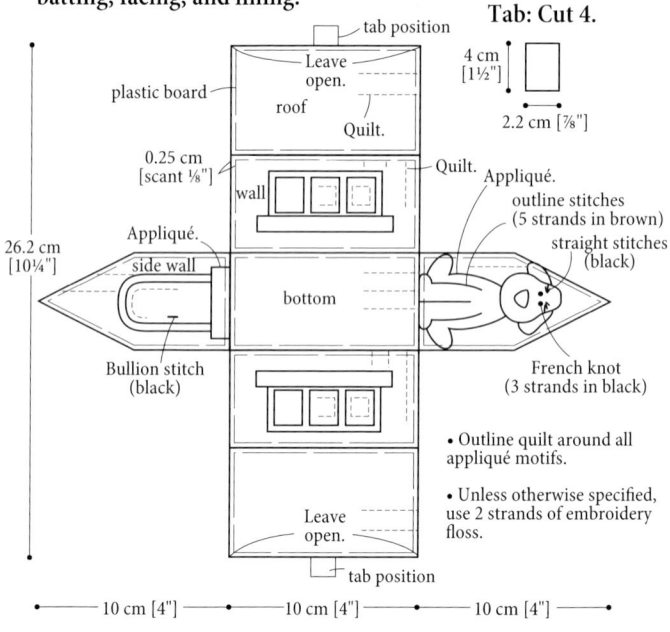

Tab: Cut 4.
4 cm [1½"]
2.2 cm [⅞"]

- Outline quilt around all appliqué motifs.
- Unless otherwise specified, use 2 strands of embroidery floss.

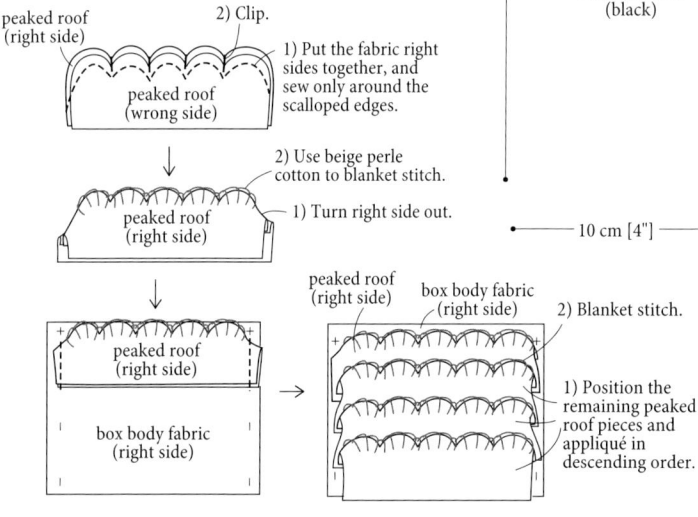

- Cut patchwork pieces for walls, bottom, and roof of box from desired fabrics, adding 0.7 cm [¼"] seam allowances. When cutting appliqués, add 0.3 to 0.4 cm [⅛"] seam allowances. Cut plastic board pieces for each wall, bottom, and roof 0.5 cm [scant ¼"] smaller than the finished dimensions of the project. Do not add seam allowances when cutting tab.
- Cut the facing, lining, and batting the size of the entire box top piece, adding 0.7 cm [¼"] seam allowances.
- Stitch appliqués and embroidery designs on each patchwork piece.
- Piece together the patchwork pieces to make the box top.

Figure 1: Making the chicken coop roof

- peaked roof (right side)
- 2) Clip.
- 1) Put the fabric right sides together, and sew only around the scalloped edges.
- peaked roof (wrong side)

↓

- peaked roof (right side)
- 2) Use beige perle cotton to blanket stitch.
- 1) Turn right side out.

↓

- peaked roof (right side)
- box body fabric (right side)
- 2) Blanket stitch.
- 1) Position the remaining peaked roof pieces and appliqué in descending order.
- box body fabric (right side)

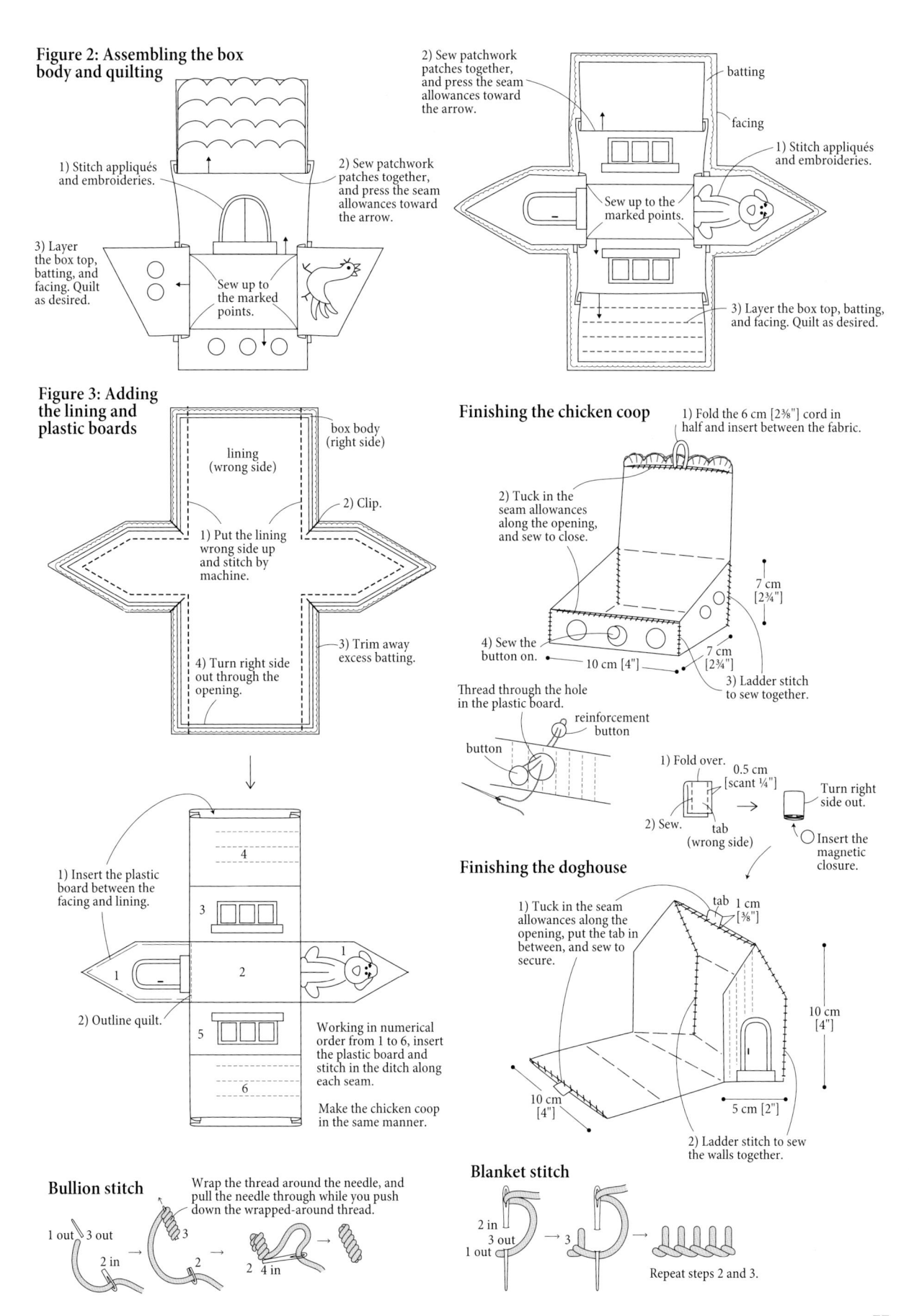

Figure 2: Assembling the box body and quilting

1) Stitch appliqués and embroideries.
2) Sew patchwork patches together, and press the seam allowances toward the arrow.
3) Layer the box top, batting, and facing. Quilt as desired.

Sew up to the marked points.

2) Sew patchwork patches together, and press the seam allowances toward the arrow.

batting
facing

1) Stitch appliqués and embroideries.

Sew up to the marked points.

3) Layer the box top, batting, and facing. Quilt as desired.

Figure 3: Adding the lining and plastic boards

box body (right side)
lining (wrong side)

1) Put the lining wrong side up and stitch by machine.
2) Clip.
3) Trim away excess batting.
4) Turn right side out through the opening.

1) Insert the plastic board between the facing and lining.
2) Outline quilt.

Working in numerical order from 1 to 6, insert the plastic board and stitch in the ditch along each seam.

Make the chicken coop in the same manner.

Finishing the chicken coop

1) Fold the 6 cm [2⅜"] cord in half and insert between the fabric.
2) Tuck in the seam allowances along the opening, and sew to close.
3) Ladder stitch to sew together.
4) Sew the button on.

7 cm [2¾"]
7 cm [2¾"]
10 cm [4"]

Thread through the hole in the plastic board.

button — reinforcement button

1) Fold over.
2) Sew.
tab (wrong side)

0.5 cm [scant ¼"]

Turn right side out.

Insert the magnetic closure.

Finishing the doghouse

1) Tuck in the seam allowances along the opening, put the tab in between, and sew to secure.

tab 1 cm [⅜"]

10 cm [4"]
10 cm [4"]
5 cm [2"]

2) Ladder stitch to sew the walls together.

Bullion stitch

1 out   3 out
2 in

Wrap the thread around the needle, and pull the needle through while you push down the wrapped-around thread.

2   4 in

Blanket stitch

2 in
3 out
1 out

Repeat steps 2 and 3.

77

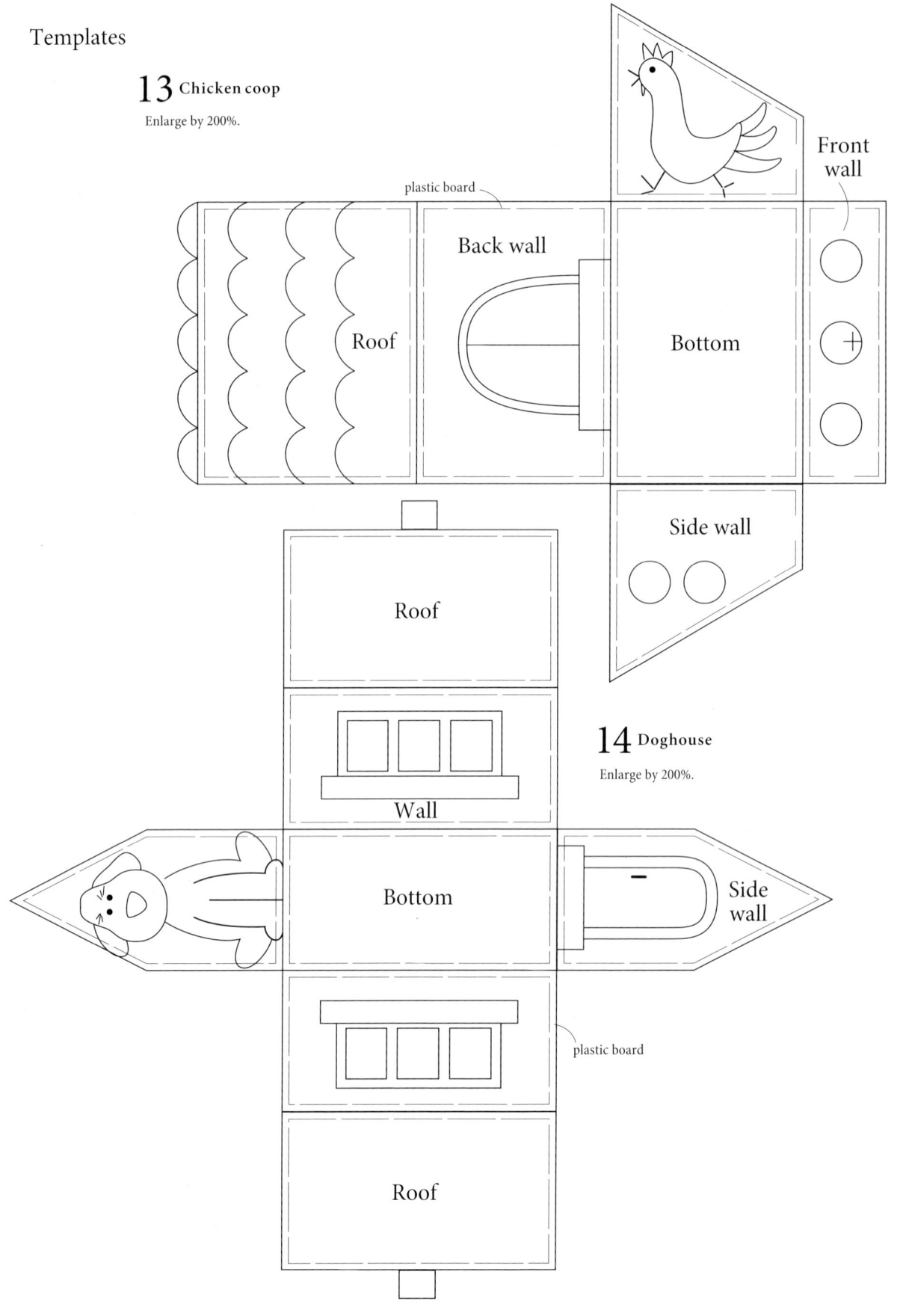

Templates

13 Chicken coop

Enlarge by 200%.

plastic board

Roof

Back wall

Bottom

Front wall

Side wall

14 Doghouse

Enlarge by 200%.

Roof

Wall

Bottom

Side wall

plastic board

Roof

78

15

Project page 28

Dragonfly Mini Quilt

Materials Needed
Cottons:
- Background print: 30 x 30 cm [12" x 12"]
- Assorted fat quarters and scraps for appliqués
- Backing: 35 x 35 cm [14" x 14"]
- Bias binding: 2.5 x 120 cm [1" x 48"]

Batting: 35 x 35 cm [14" x 14"]
Embroidery floss in various colors

Instructions
1 Stitch appliqués and embroideries on the background to make the top.
2 Layer the top prepared in step 1 with batting and backing. Quilt as desired.
3 Sew the binding to the edges of the quilt prepared in step 2. Turn the quilt over; stitch the binding to the back of the quilt.

Outline stitch
1 out, 3 out, 2 in, 3
Repeat steps 2 and 3.

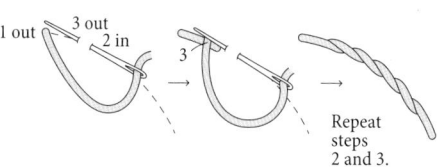

Lazy daisy stitch
3 out, 1 out, 2 in, 4 in

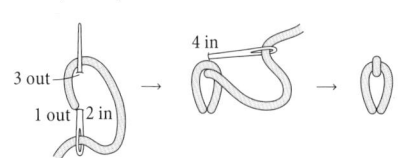

Colonial knot
1 out, 1, 2 in

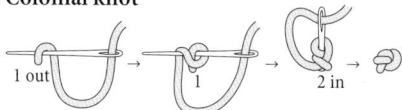

Dimensional diagram
Enlarge the templates by 200%

outline stitches (1 strand each in white and navy)

lazy daisy stitches (3 strands in dark green)

Quilt 0.3 cm [⅛"] from the edge.

Appliqué.

outline stitches (4 strands in dark gray)

colonial knot (6 strands in gray)

Quilt following the pattern of the fabric.

colonial knot (2 strands in white, 4 strands in navy)

26 cm [10¼"]

Outline quilt around all appliqué and embroidery motifs.

26 cm [10¼"]

16 Round Case

Project page 30

Materials Needed

Cottons:
- Assorted fat quarters and scraps for patchwork, case side, and bottom
- Multicolored plaid for case side backing, lid lining, and case bottom lining: 30 x 30 cm [12" x 12"]
- Bias binding: 3.5 x 35 cm [1⅜" x 14"]
- Facing: 20 x 10 cm [8" x 4"]

Extra heavyweight interfacing: 20 x 10 cm [8" x 4"]
Batting: 30 x 30 cm [12" x 12"]
3 cm [1¼"] wide linen tape or ribbon: 20 cm [8"]
20 cm [8"] zipper
Beads (1.3 [½"] and 0.4 cm [⅛"] in diameter): 1 each
1 button (0.6 cm [¼"] in diameter)
Plastic board or template plastic

Instructions

1 Sew patchwork pieces together to make the lid.
2 Layer the prepared lid with batting and facing and quilt as desired. Make a hole in the middle of the plastic board and wrap with the quilted lid (figure 1).
3 Prepare the lid lining and case bottom lining (figure 2).
4 Shorten zipper to fit (7⅞"). Make a loop with the zipper and sandwich the zipper ends with the two pieces of linen ribbon (figure 3).
5 Ladder stitch the lid to one edge of the zipper (figure 4).
6 Position the prepared lid lining on the lid wrong side and blindstitch in place (figure 5).
7 Sew together the short ends of the quilted case side. With right sides together, join the case side and bottom (figure 6).

Case lid: Cut 1 each for top, batting, facing, lining, extra heavyweight interfacing, and plastic board.

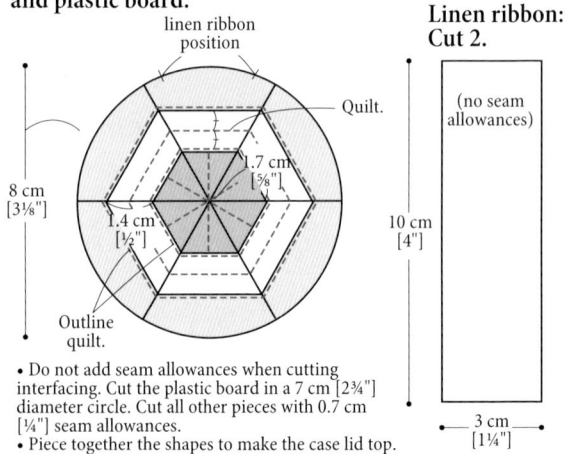

- Do not add seam allowances when cutting interfacing. Cut the plastic board in a 7 cm [2¾"] diameter circle. Cut all other pieces with 0.7 cm [¼"] seam allowances.
- Piece together the shapes to make the case lid top.
- For the case side and bottom, make a quilt sandwich with top, batting, and backing; quilt.

Linen ribbon: Cut 2. (no seam allowances) 10 cm [4"] × 3 cm [1¼"]

Case side: Cut 1 for top, batting, and backing.
Quilt following the pattern of the fabric.
Place on fold. 4 cm [1½"] × 24.5 cm [9⅝"]

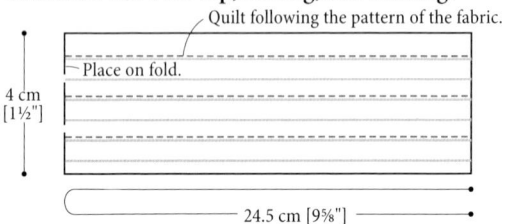

Case bottom: Cut 1 for top, batting, facing, lining, and extra heavyweight interfacing.
8 cm [3⅛"]
Quilt as desired.

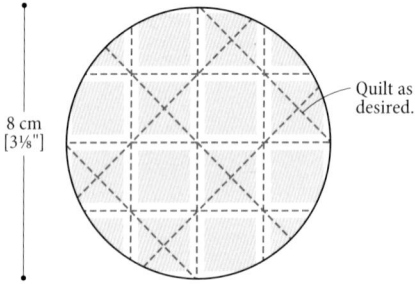

Figure 1: Assembling the lid
lid top (right side)
Sew with a running stitch and gather the seam allowances around the board.
plastic board
Make a hole at the center.
(wrong side)
facing
batting

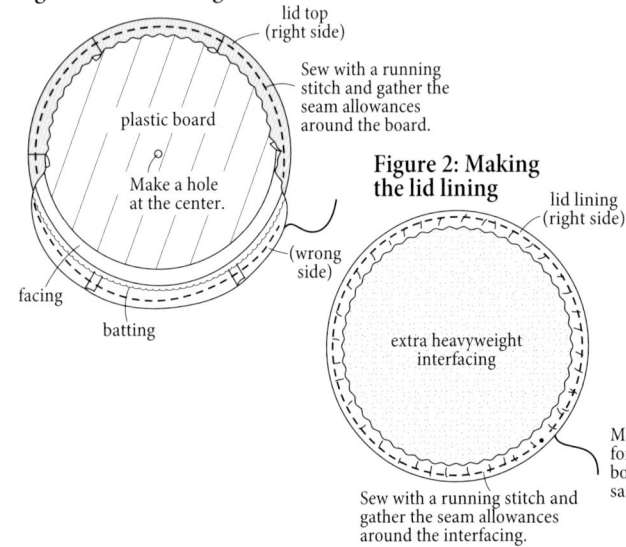

Figure 2: Making the lid lining
lid lining (right side)
extra heavyweight interfacing
Sew with a running stitch and gather the seam allowances around the interfacing.
Make the lining for the case bottom in the same manner.

Figure 3: Preparing the zipper
zipper (wrong side)
1 cm [⅜"]
3 cm [1¼"]
(right side)
linen ribbon (right side)
6 cm [2⅜"]

Make sure that the circumference of the zipper loop is the same as that of the finished case side (24.5 cm [9⅝"]).

Sandwich the zipper ends with the two lengths of linen ribbon. Sew along the linen ribbon as shown to make a zipper loop.

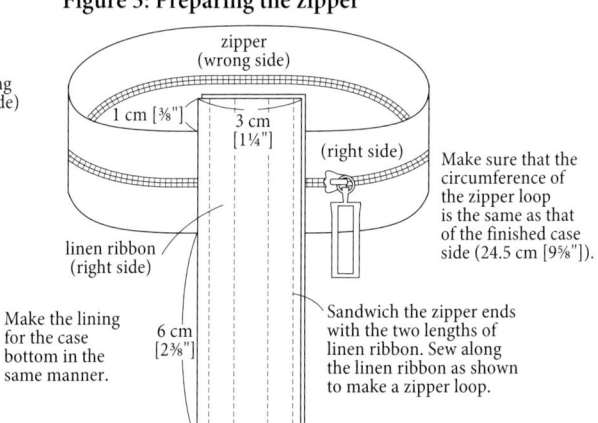

8 Position the prepared case bottom lining on the case bottom wrong side and blindstitch in place. Bind the case opening.

9 Backstitch the bound edge of the case side to the remaining edge of the zipper tape. Blindstitch the linen ribbon over the seam allowances on the case side.

10 Attach beads to the lid center.

Figure 4: Joining the lid and zipper

Ladder stitch the lid to one edge of the zipper loop.

lid (right side)

zipper (right side)

linen ribbon (right side)

Figure 5: Adding the lid lining

lid lining (right side)

× Position the lid lining on the lid, sandwiching the linen ribbon pieces, and blindstitch.

zipper (wrong side)

linen ribbon (wrong side)

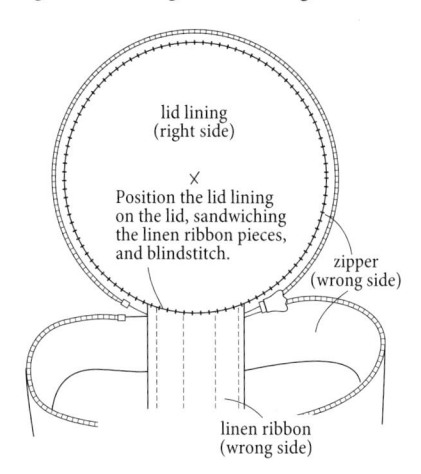

Figure 6: Assembling the case

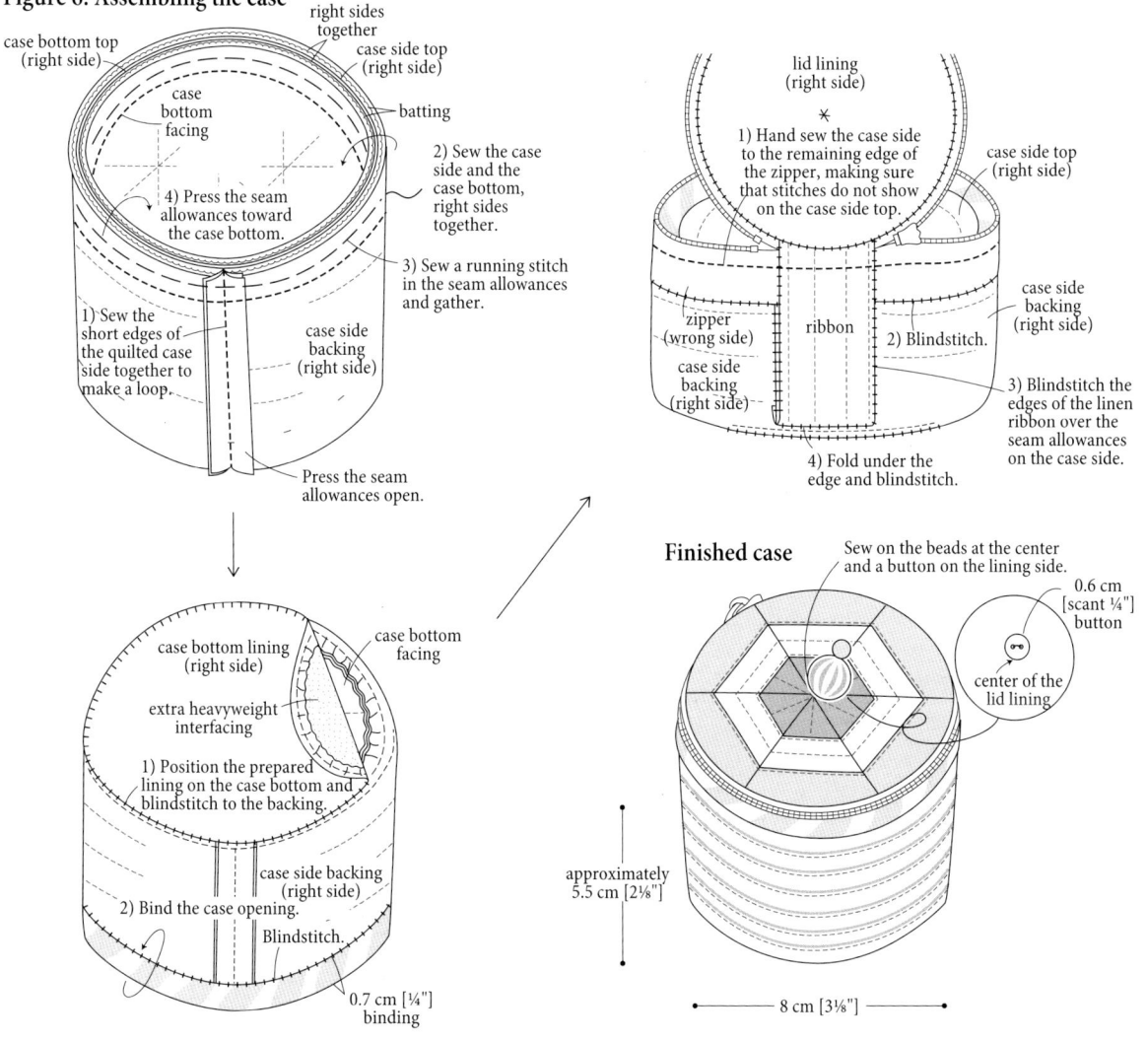

case bottom top (right side)

right sides together

case side top (right side)

case bottom facing

batting

2) Sew the case side and the case bottom, right sides together.

3) Sew a running stitch in the seam allowances and gather.

4) Press the seam allowances toward the case bottom.

1) Sew the short edges of the quilted case side together to make a loop.

case side backing (right side)

Press the seam allowances open.

case bottom lining (right side)

case bottom facing

extra heavyweight interfacing

1) Position the prepared lining on the case bottom and blindstitch to the backing.

case side backing (right side)

2) Bind the case opening.

Blindstitch.

0.7 cm [¼"] binding

lid lining (right side)

✳ 1) Hand sew the case side to the remaining edge of the zipper, making sure that stitches do not show on the case side top.

case side top (right side)

case side backing (right side)

zipper (wrong side)

ribbon

2) Blindstitch.

case side backing (right side)

3) Blindstitch the edges of the linen ribbon over the seam allowances on the case side.

4) Fold under the edge and blindstitch.

Finished case

Sew on the beads at the center and a button on the lining side.

0.6 cm [scant ¼"] button

center of the lid lining

approximately 5.5 cm [2⅛"]

8 cm [3⅛"]

17
Coin Purse

Project page 32 Full-size templates on page 103

Materials Needed
Cottons:
- Assorted fat quarters and scraps for patchwork and magnetic closures
- Blue print for purse body B: 15 x 10 cm [6" x 4"]
- Backing: 25 x 20 cm [10" x 8"]

Batting: 25 x 20 cm [10" x 8"]
2 pairs sew-on magnetic closures (1 cm [3/8"] in diameter)

Instructions
1 Sew patchwork pieces together to make the purse body A top.
2 Put the top for purse body pieces A and B individually with backing right sides together; put batting on top (figures 1 and 2). Sew all around except for an opening to turn right side out.
3 Turn the pieces prepared in step 2 right side out. Quilt as desired.
4 Wrap magnetic closures with fabric; sew in place (figure 3).
5 Whipstitch purse body pieces A and B together.

Purse body A: Cut 1 for top, batting, and backing.

3.5 cm [1 3/8"]
0.7 cm [1/4"]
0.7 cm [1/4"]
1 cm [3/8"]
0.7 cm [1/4"]
10 cm [4"]
1 cm [3/8"]
12.5 cm [5"]

Machine sew 0.1 cm [1/16"] from the edge after quilting.

Stitch in the ditch around all patchwork pieces.

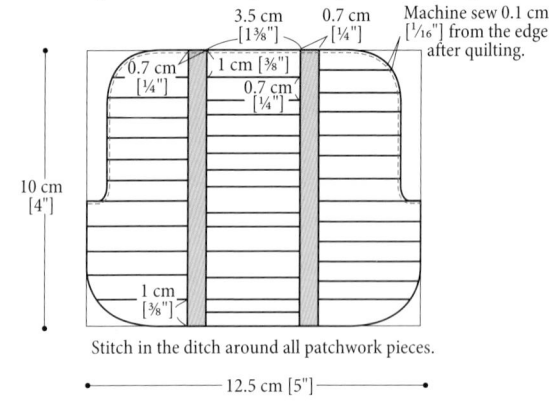

Purse body B: Cut 1 for top, batting, and backing.

Machine sew 0.1 cm [1/16"] from the edge.
Quilt every 0.7 cm [1/4"] or 0.5 cm [scant 1/4"].
4.5 cm [1 3/4"]
3.3 cm [1 1/4"]
1.2 cm [1/2"]
12.5 cm [5"]
1 cm [3/8"] magnetic closure wrapped in fabric

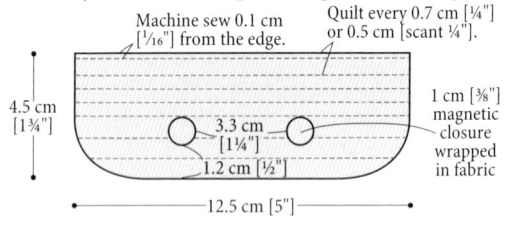

Figure 1: Preparing purse body A

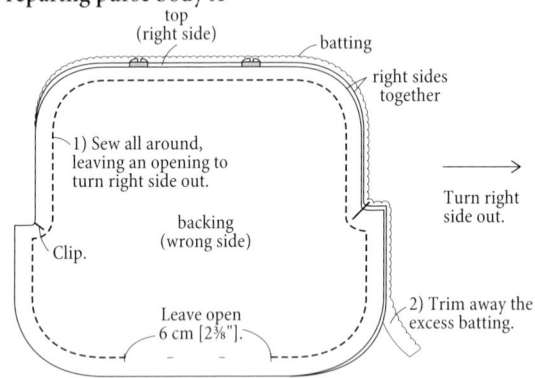

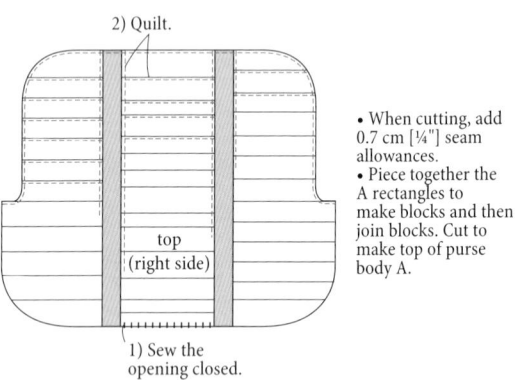

top (right side)
batting
right sides together
1) Sew all around, leaving an opening to turn right side out.
backing (wrong side)
Clip.
Leave open 6 cm [2 3/8"].
Turn right side out.
2) Trim away the excess batting.

2) Quilt.
top (right side)
1) Sew the opening closed.

- When cutting, add 0.7 cm [1/4"] seam allowances.
- Piece together the A rectangles to make blocks and then join blocks. Cut to make top of purse body A.

Figure 2: Preparing purse body B

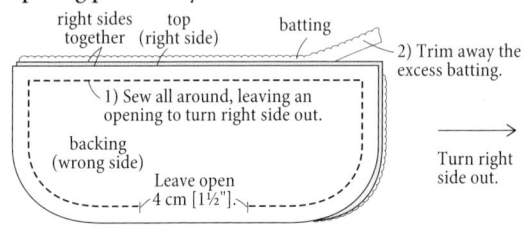

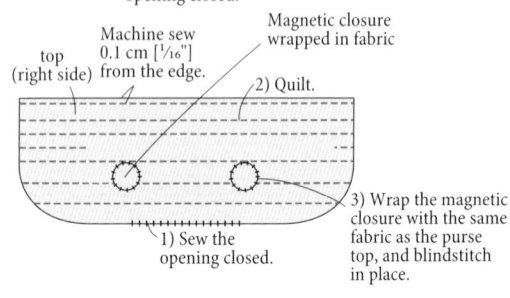

right sides together
top (right side)
batting
2) Trim away the excess batting.
1) Sew all around, leaving an opening to turn right side out.
backing (wrong side)
Leave open 4 cm [1 1/2"].
Turn right side out.

Machine sew 0.1 cm [1/16"] from the edge.
top (right side)
Magnetic closure wrapped in fabric
2) Quilt.
1) Sew the opening closed.
3) Wrap the magnetic closure with the same fabric as the purse top, and blindstitch in place.

Figure 3: Assembling the purse

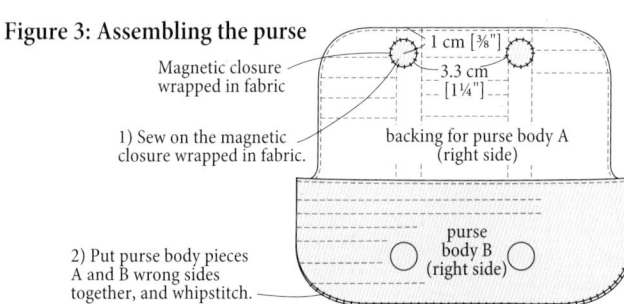

Magnetic closure wrapped in fabric
1 cm [3/8"]
3.3 cm [1 1/4"]
1) Sew on the magnetic closure wrapped in fabric.
backing for purse body A (right side)
purse body B (right side)
2) Put purse body pieces A and B wrong sides together, and whipstitch.

Finished purse

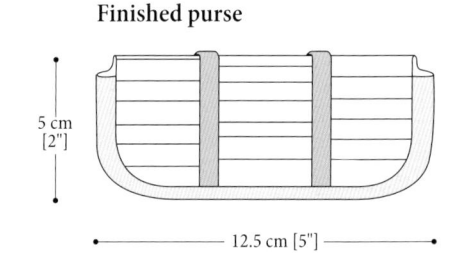

5 cm [2"]
12.5 cm [5"]

82

18 Sewing Kit

Project page 34

Materials Needed

Cottons:
- Assorted fat quarters and scraps for patchwork
- Lining: 15 x 13 cm [6" x 5½"]

Tulle: 13 x 9 cm [5½" x 3½"]

Batting: 15 x 13 cm [6" x 5½"]

2.5 cm [1"] wide linen tape or ribbon: 25 cm [10"]

1 pair sew-through metal purse clasps (12 x 6 cm [4¾" x 2⅜"])

Embroidery floss in ecru

Instructions

1 Stitch patchwork pieces together to make four Log Cabin blocks. Join the blocks and remaining patchwork pieces to make the sewing kit body top.

2 Enclose the long edges of the inside pocket with linen ribbon; sew in place. Position the pocket on the lining and sew on the marked center line.

3 Position the sewing kit top on the batting, then place the lining/pocket piece prepared in step 2 on top, right sides together. Sew all around, leaving an opening to turn right side out.

4 Turn right side out and sew the opening closed. Insert the main body in the metal clasps; sew.

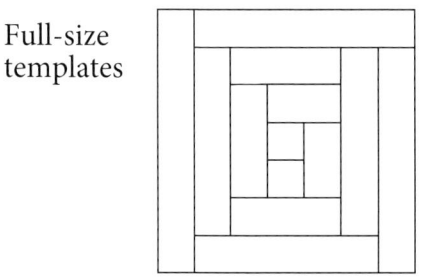

Sewing kit body: Cut 1 for top, lining, and batting.

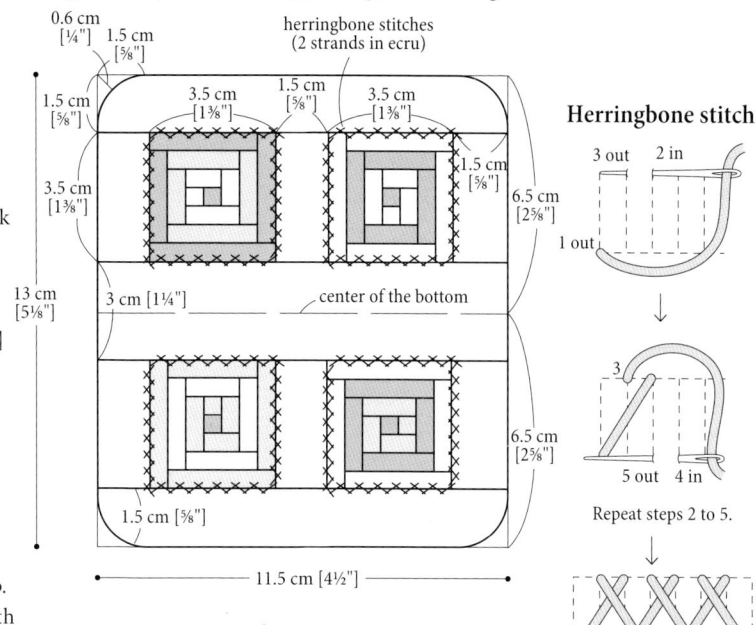

Herringbone stitch

Inside pocket: Cut 1 from tulle.

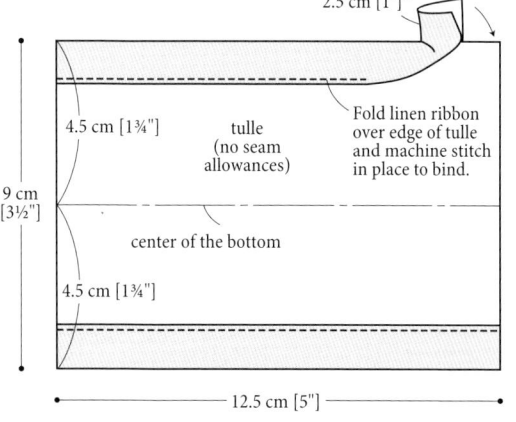

- When cutting patchwork pieces for pieced sewing kit body top, add 0.7 cm [¼"] seam allowances. When cutting batting and lining, add 1 cm [⅜"] seam allowances. Do not add seam allowances when cutting tulle.
- Piece together the strips to make Log Cabin blocks. Then join the blocks and remaining patchwork pieces to make the sewing kit top.
- Embroider the sewing kit top as shown.

Full-size templates

Figure 1: Assembling the sewing kit

Machine sew along the marked center point of the bottom on the lining and inside pocket.

Leave open 8 cm [3⅛"].

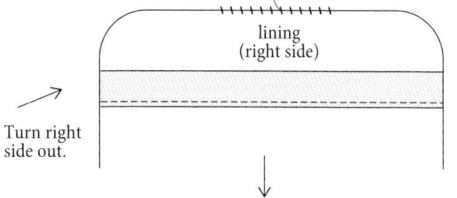

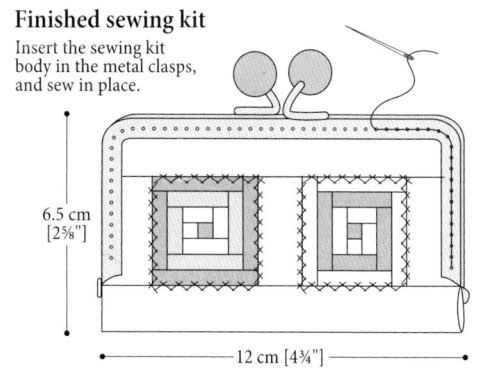

Sew all around.

Sew the opening closed.

Turn right side out.

Finished sewing kit

Insert the sewing kit body in the metal clasps, and sew in place.

19 Watermelon Pincushions

Project page 35
Full-size templates on page 85

Instructions

1 Stitch the solid white rind appliqués to the red check main body (figure 1).
2 For pincushions B and C, fold the main body in half right sides together, stitching between the marks.
3 Sew the main body and bottom right sides together, leaving an opening to turn right side out.
4 Turn right side out. Stuff with cotton; sew to close the opening.
5 Sew on buttons or beads.

Materials Needed

For Pincushion A
Cottons:
- Red check: 16 x 16 cm [7" x 7"]
- Solid white: 16 x 16 cm [7" x 7"]
- Green check: 30 x 30 cm [12" x 12"]

10 buttons (0.8 cm [¼"] in diameter)
Cotton stuffing

For Pincushion B
Cottons:
- Red check: 15 x 15 cm [6" x 6"]
- Solid white: 15 x 15 cm [6" x 6"]
- Green check: 15 x 15 cm [6" x 6"]

8 beads (0.4 cm [⅛"] in diameter)
Cotton stuffing

For Pincushion C
Cottons:
- Red check: 15 x 15 cm [6" x 6"]
- Solid white: 15 x 15 cm [6" x 6"]
- Green check: 12 x 12 cm [3" x 3"]

6 beads (0.4 cm [⅛"] in diameter)
Cotton stuffing

Main body A: Cut 1 from red check and 1 rind appliqué from solid white.

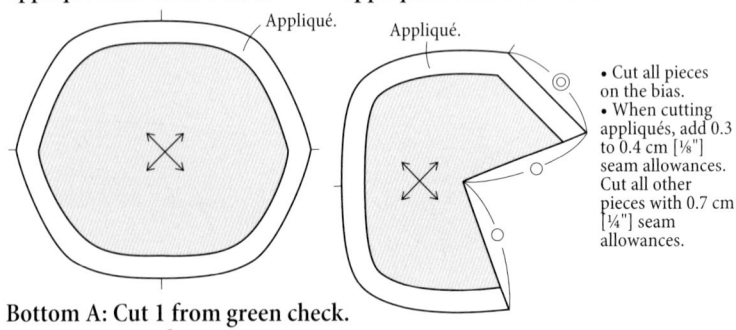

Main body B: Cut 1 from red check and 1 rind appliqué from solid white.

- Cut all pieces on the bias.
- When cutting appliqués, add 0.3 to 0.4 cm [⅛"] seam allowances. Cut all other pieces with 0.7 cm [¼"] seam allowances.

Bottom A: Cut 1 from green check.
Leave open 3.5 cm [1⅜"].

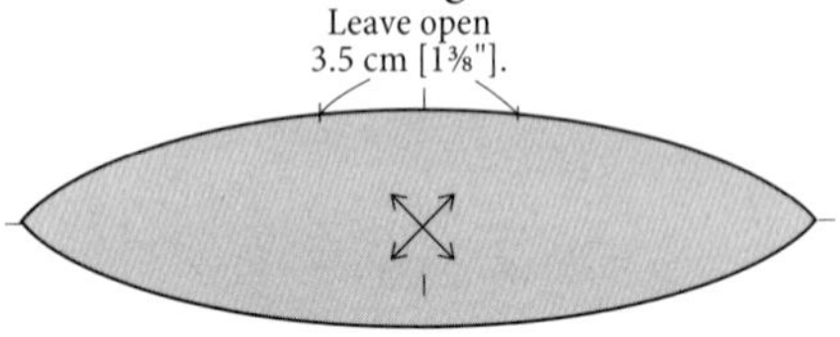

Bottom B: Cut 1 from green check.
Leave open 3.5 cm [1⅜"].

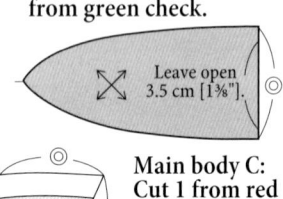

Main body C: Cut 1 from red check and 1 rind appliqué from solid white.

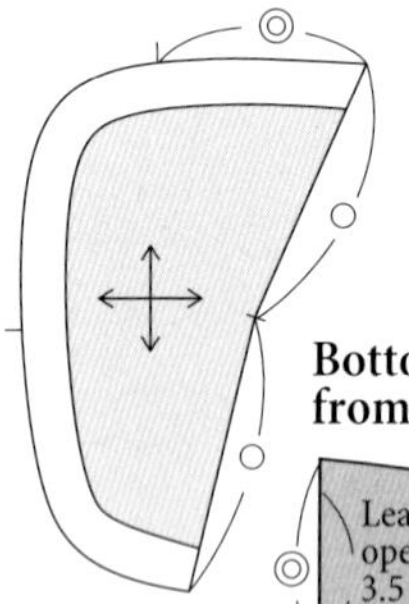

Bottom C: Cut 1 from green check.
Leave open 3.5 cm [1⅜"].

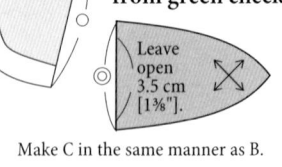

Make C in the same manner as B.

Figure 1: Sewing appliqués to A

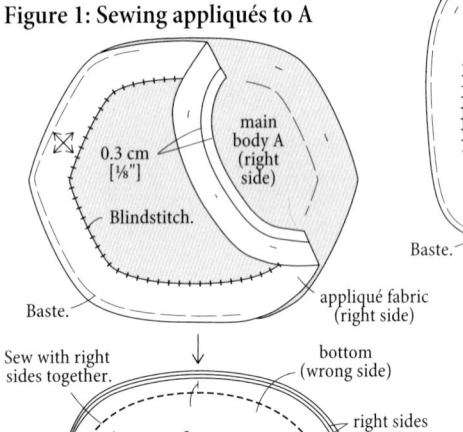

Sewing appliqués to B

Figure 2: Sewing the main body and bottom together

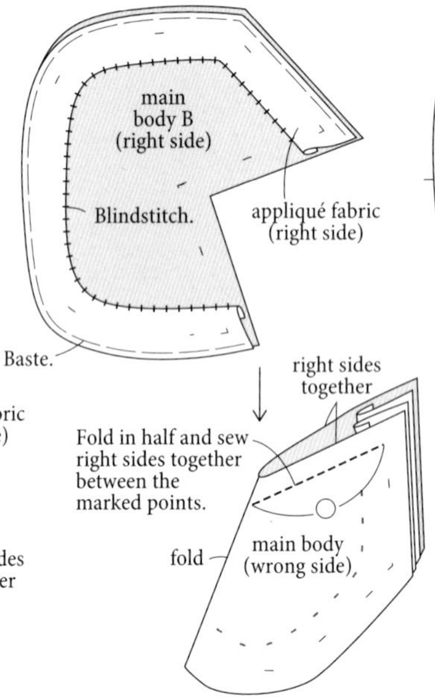

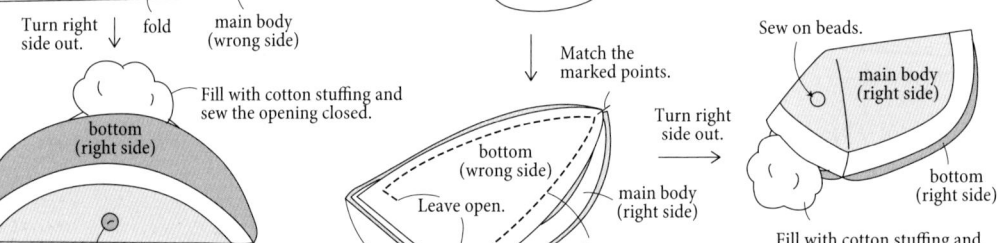

Key
○ Edges to match when sewing main body
◎ Edges to match when joining bottom to main body

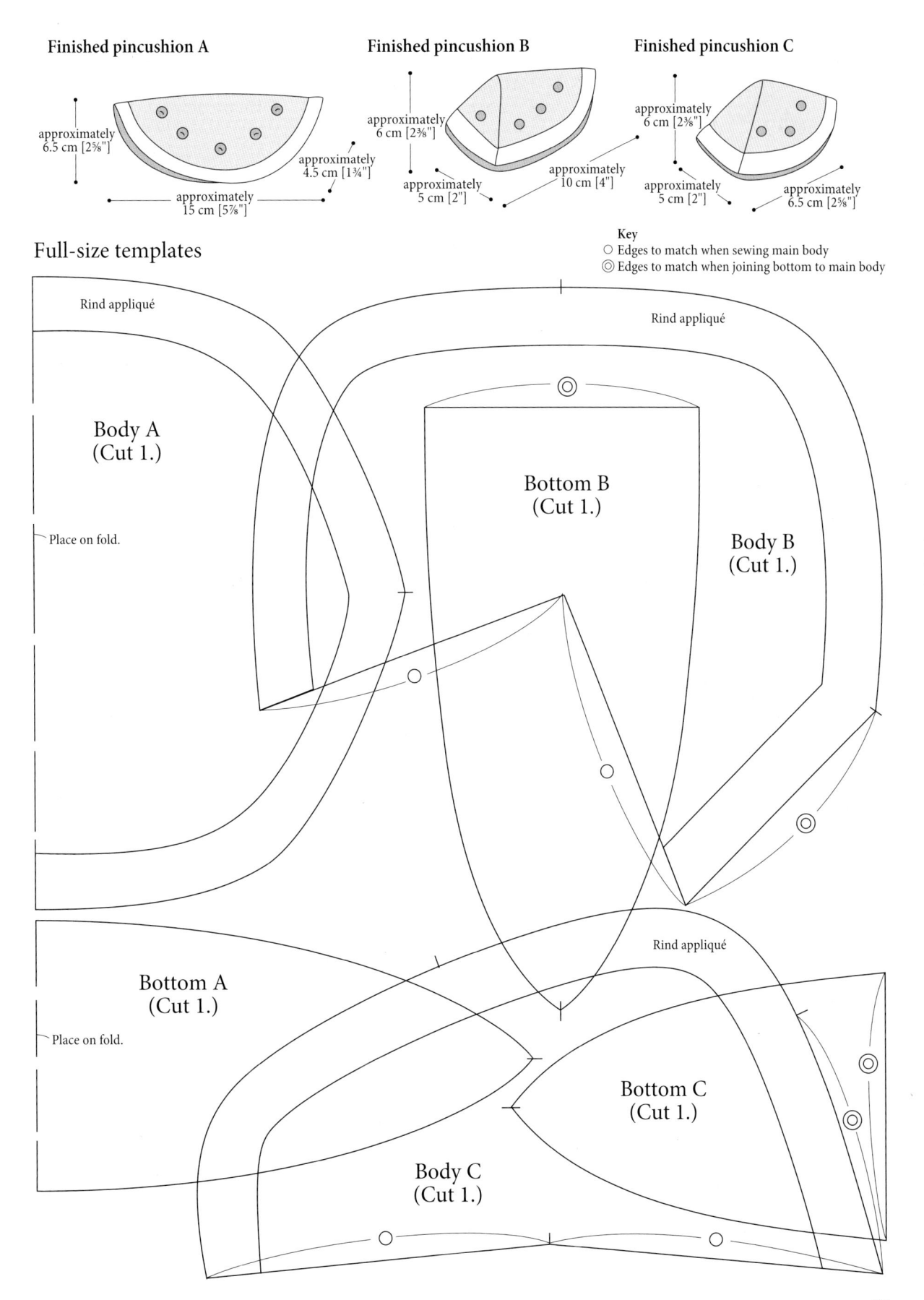

Finished pincushion A
approximately 6.5 cm [2⅝"]
approximately 4.5 cm [1¾"]
approximately 15 cm [5⅞"]

Finished pincushion B
approximately 6 cm [2⅜"]
approximately 5 cm [2"]
approximately 10 cm [4"]

Finished pincushion C
approximately 6 cm [2⅜"]
approximately 5 cm [2"]
approximately 6.5 cm [2⅝"]

Full-size templates

Key
○ Edges to match when sewing main body
◎ Edges to match when joining bottom to main body

Rind appliqué

Body A (Cut 1.)
Place on fold.

Bottom B (Cut 1.)

Body B (Cut 1.)

Rind appliqué

Bottom A (Cut 1.)
Place on fold.

Rind appliqué

Bottom C (Cut 1.)

Body C (Cut 1.)

85

20
Buggy Coin Purse

Project page 36
Full-size templates on page 87

Materials Needed

Cottons:
- Assorted fat quarters and scraps for purse front background and appliqués
- Multicolored print for purse back and divider:
  80 x 20 cm [32" x 8"]
- Lining: 20 x 15 cm [8" x 6"]
- Facing: 30 x 20 cm [12" x 8"]
- Bias-cut binding: 3.5 x 70 cm [1⅜" x 28"]

Batting: 30 x 20 cm [12" x 8"]
Fusible interfacing: 40 x 30 cm [16" x 12"]
70 cm [28"] free-style zipper; shorten to fit (27½")
Decorative zipper pull
1.5 cm [⅝"] wide ribbon: 10 cm [4"]
Embroidery floss in various colors

Instructions

1 Stitch appliqués and embroideries on the background to make the purse front top.

2 Layer the piece prepared in step 1 and purse back top individually with batting and facing. Quilt as desired.

3 Sew the purse front and back together, bind the seam allowances, then baste the lining on top (figure 1).

4 Assemble the divider sides and center, and join (figures 2 and 3).

5 Attach the divider to the lining and bind the edges (figure 4).

6 Sew in the zipper and bind the zipper tape end (figure 5).

Purse front: Cut 1 each for top, batting, and facing.
- Refer to the full-size templates for embroideries.
- Outline quilt around all appliqué motifs.

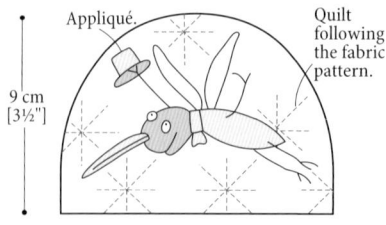

9 cm [3½"]
Appliqué.
Quilt following the fabric pattern.

Purse back: Cut 1 each for top, batting, and facing.
10 cm [4"]
1.3 cm [½"] crosshatch machine quilting
13 cm [5⅛"]

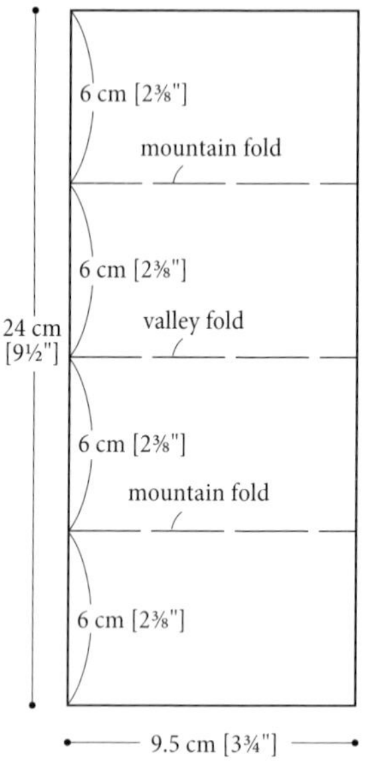

Lining: Cut 1 each for top and interfacing.
18 cm [7⅛"]
Place on fold.
13 cm [5⅛"]

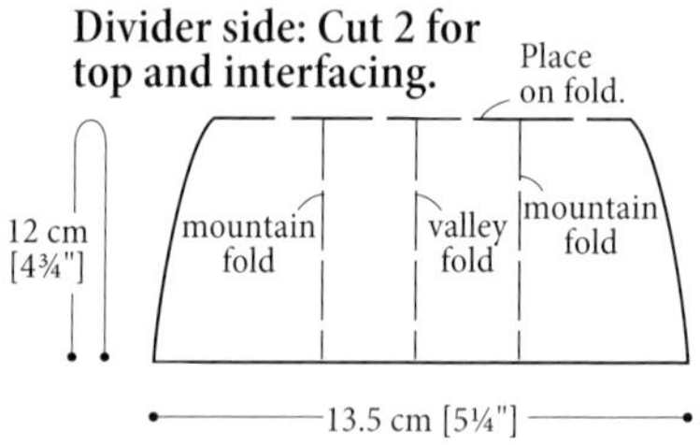

- When cutting appliqués, add 0.3 to 0.4 cm [⅛"] seam allowances. Do not add seam allowances when cutting interfacing. When cutting facing for the purse front, add 2 cm [¾"] seam allowances to the bottom edge only. Cut all other edges and pieces with 1 cm [⅜"] seam allowances.
- Stitch appliqués and embroidery designs on the purse front top.
- For the purse front and back, make a quilt sandwich with top, batting, and facing; machine quilt.

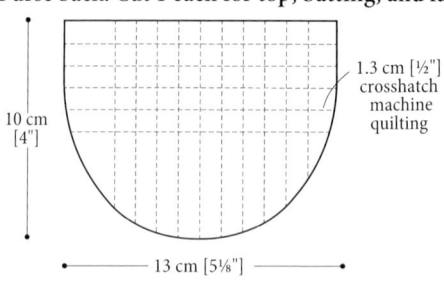

Divider center: Cut 1 each for top and interfacing.
6 cm [2⅜"] mountain fold
6 cm [2⅜"] valley fold
24 cm [9½"]
6 cm [2⅜"] mountain fold
6 cm [2⅜"]
9.5 cm [3¾"]

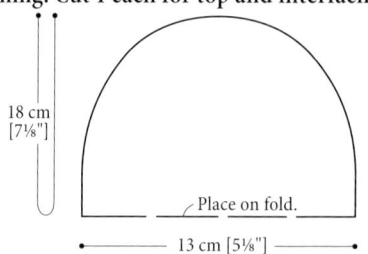

Divider side: Cut 2 for top and interfacing. Place on fold.
12 cm [4¾"]
mountain fold, valley fold, mountain fold
13.5 cm [5¼"]

Figure 1: Assembling the purse

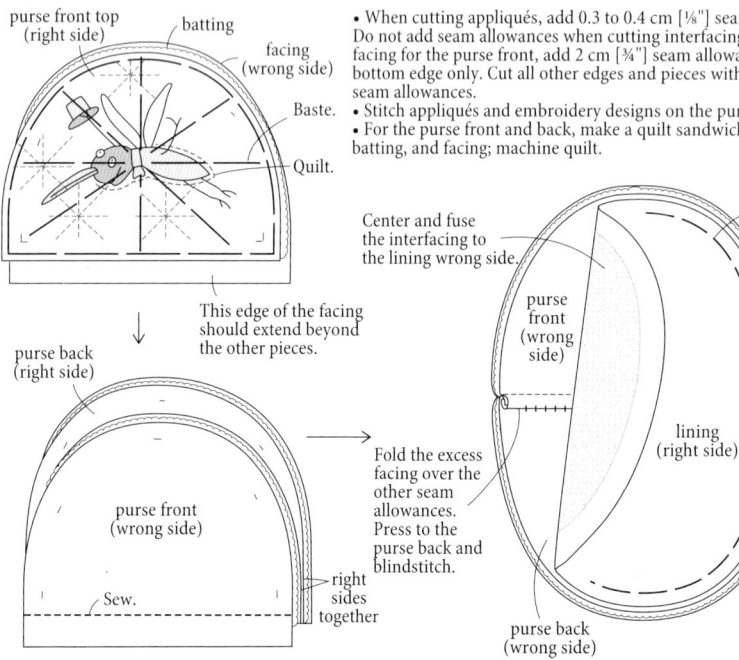

purse front top (right side)
batting
facing (wrong side)
Baste.
Quilt.

purse back (right side)
purse front (wrong side)
Sew.
right sides together

This edge of the facing should extend beyond the other pieces.

Center and fuse the interfacing to the lining wrong side.

purse front (wrong side)
lining (right side)
purse back (wrong side)
Baste.

Fold the excess facing over the other seam allowances. Press to the purse back and blindstitch.

Figure 2: Making the center divider

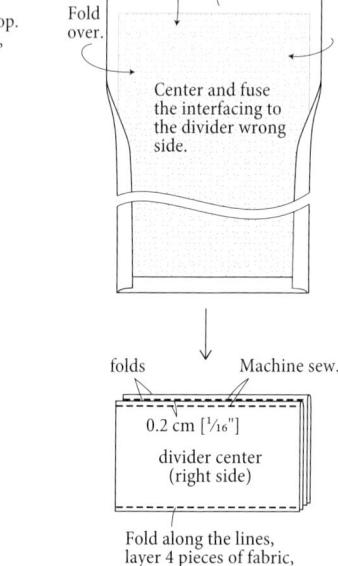

divider center (wrong side)
Fold over.
Center and fuse the interfacing to the divider wrong side.

folds
Machine sew.
0.2 cm [1/16"]
divider center (right side)

Fold along the lines, layer 4 pieces of fabric, and machine sew.

Figure 3: Assembling the divider sides

Center and fuse interfacing to one half of the divider wrong side.

divider side (wrong side)

divider side (right side)

fold 0.2 cm [1/16"]

Machine sew 0.2 cm [1/16"] from the edge.

Fold.

Machine sew.

Sandwich the divider center and machine sew.

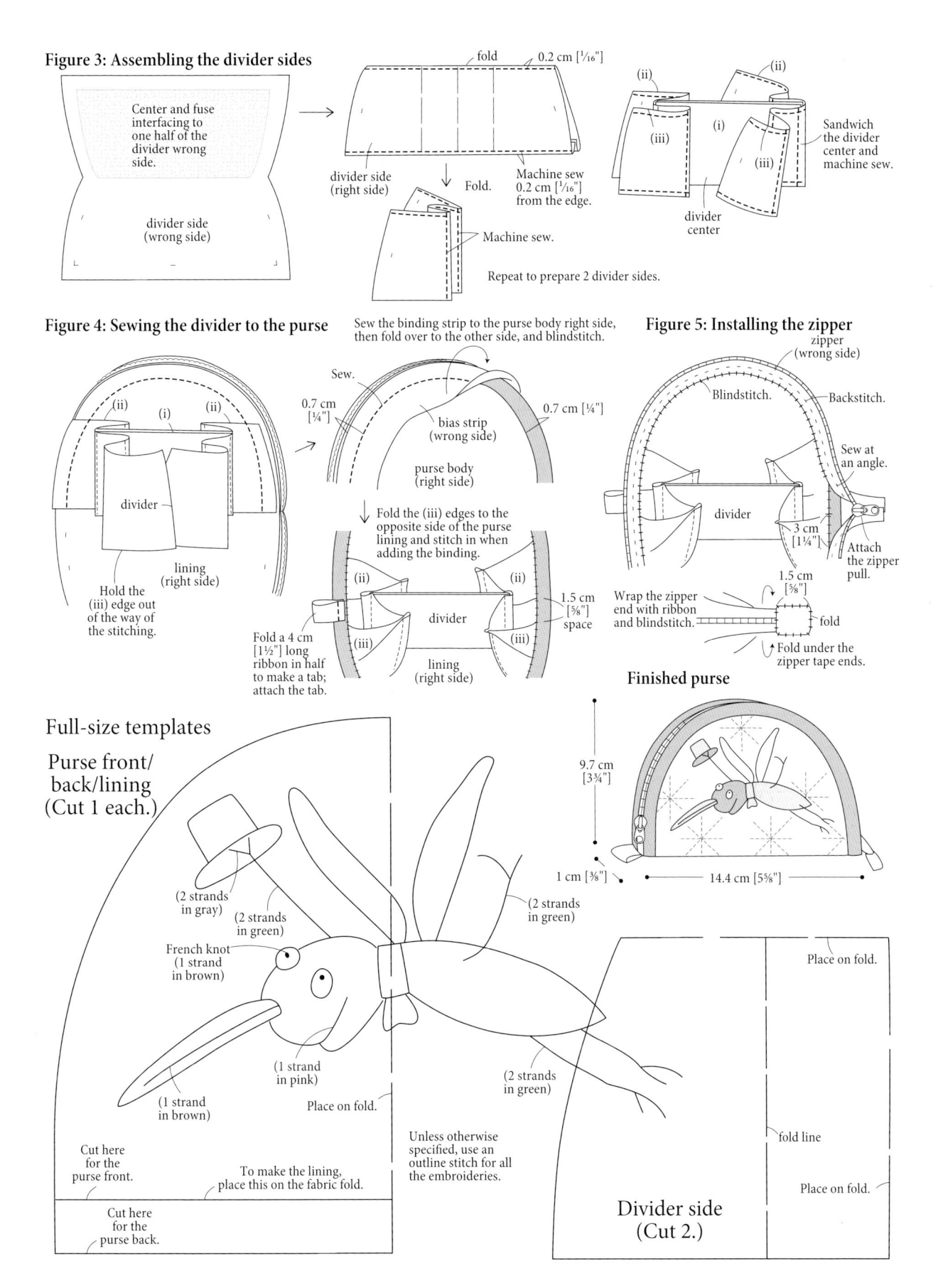

divider center

Repeat to prepare 2 divider sides.

Figure 4: Sewing the divider to the purse

divider

lining (right side)

Hold the (iii) edge out of the way of the stitching.

Sew the binding strip to the purse body right side, then fold over to the other side, and blindstitch.

Sew.

0.7 cm [1/4"]

bias strip (wrong side)

purse body (right side)

0.7 cm [1/4"]

Fold the (iii) edges to the opposite side of the purse lining and stitch in when adding the binding.

Fold a 4 cm [1½"] long ribbon in half to make a tab; attach the tab.

divider

lining (right side)

1.5 cm [5/8"] space

Figure 5: Installing the zipper

zipper (wrong side)

Blindstitch.   Backstitch.

Sew at an angle.

divider

3 cm [1¼"]

Attach the zipper pull.

Wrap the zipper end with ribbon and blindstitch.

1.5 cm [5/8"]

fold

Fold under the zipper tape ends.

Finished purse

9.7 cm [3¾"]

1 cm [3/8"]   14.4 cm [5⅝"]

Full-size templates

Purse front/back/lining (Cut 1 each.)

(2 strands in gray)
(2 strands in green)
(2 strands in green)
French knot (1 strand in brown)
(1 strand in pink)
(1 strand in brown)
(2 strands in green)

Place on fold.

Cut here for the purse front.

To make the lining, place this on the fabric fold.

Cut here for the purse back.

Unless otherwise specified, use an outline stitch for all the embroideries.

Divider side (Cut 2.)

Place on fold.

fold line

Place on fold.

21
Whale Bag

Project page 38
Templates on page 89

Materials Needed
Cottons:
- Blue yarn-dye for bag body: 40 x 20 cm [16" x 8"]
- Light blue solids for appliqués: 15 x 10 cm [6" x 4"]
- Backing and pocket: 40 x 30 cm [16" x 12"]
- Bag bottom and facing: 20 x 10 cm [8" x 4"] each
- Bias binding: 3.5 x 35 cm [1⅜" x 14"]

Batting: 40 x 30 cm [16" x 12"]
Fusible interfacing and heavyweight double-sided fusible web: 15 x 5 cm [6" x 2"] each
0.5 cm [scant ¼"] wide flat cord: 12 cm [4¾"]
2 cm [¾"] wide twill tape: 30 cm [12"]
Handle with hooks on ends: 1 piece
Embroidery floss in various colors

Instructions
1 Referring to the diagram above right and the embroidery designs on page 89, stitch appliqués and embroideries on the bag body top.
2 Layer the prepared bag body top with batting and backing; quilt to make the bag body. Sew the bag body to make a loop; use the backing to bind the seam allowances (figure 1).
3 Attach the pocket (figure 2).
4 Center and fuse the fusible web to the bag bottom top. Layer the bag bottom top with batting and facing; quilt. Then sew the bag body and bottom together (figure 3). Center and fuse the heavyweight interfacing to the backing for the bottom. Fuse and sew over the facing.
5 Attach tabs to the bag opening; bind. Attach bag handle (figure 4).

Bag body: Cut 1 each for bag body background, batting, and backing.

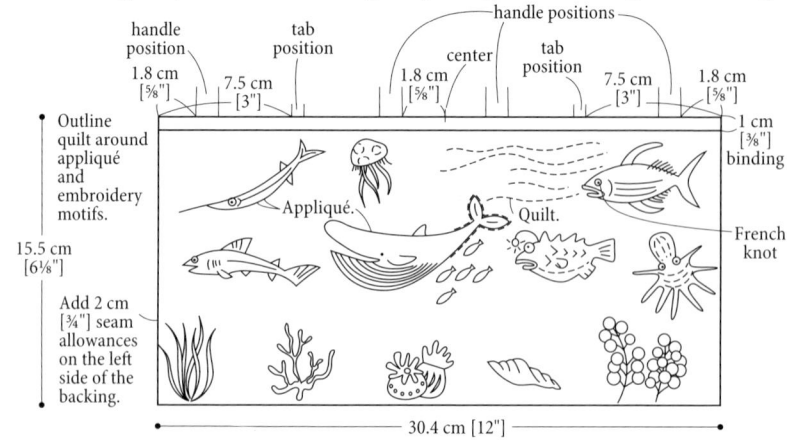

- When cutting appliqués, add 0.3 to 0.4 cm [⅛"] seam allowances. Do not add seam allowances when cutting interfacing or fusible web. When cutting backing, add 2 cm [¾"] seam allowances to the left side edge only. Cut all other edges and pieces with 0.7 cm [¼"] seam allowances.
- Stitch appliqués and embroidery designs on the bag body top.

Bag bottom: Cut 1 each for top, batting, interfacing, heavyweight fusible web, and facing.

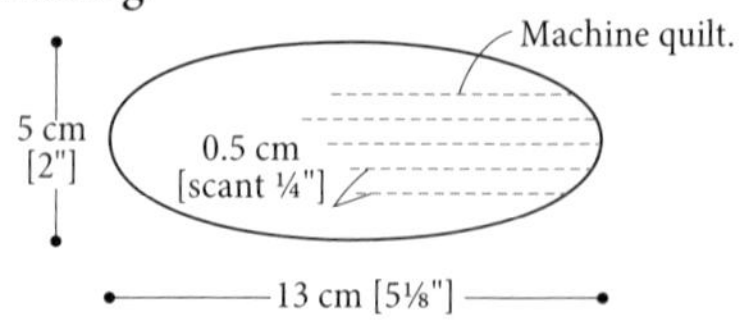

Pocket: Cut 1.

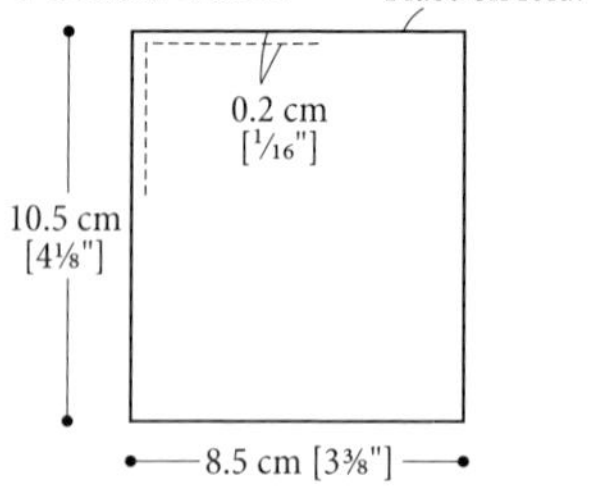

Figure 1: Sewing the bag body

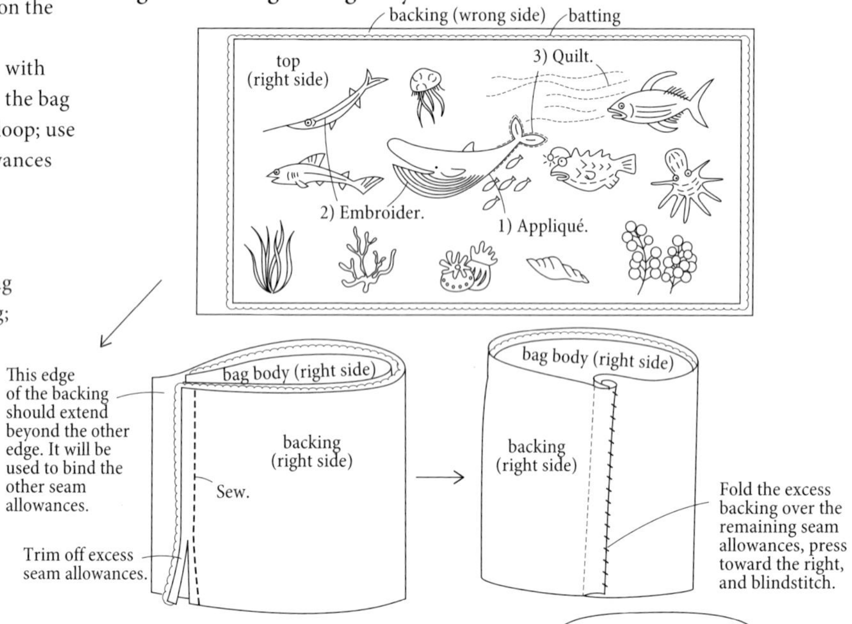

Figure 2: Sewing on the pocket

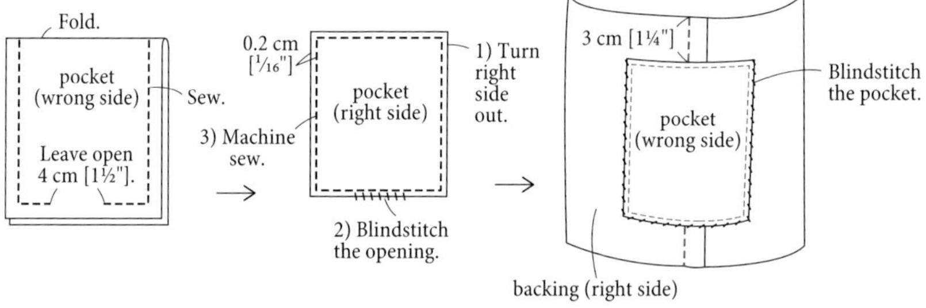

Figure 3: Making the bag bottom

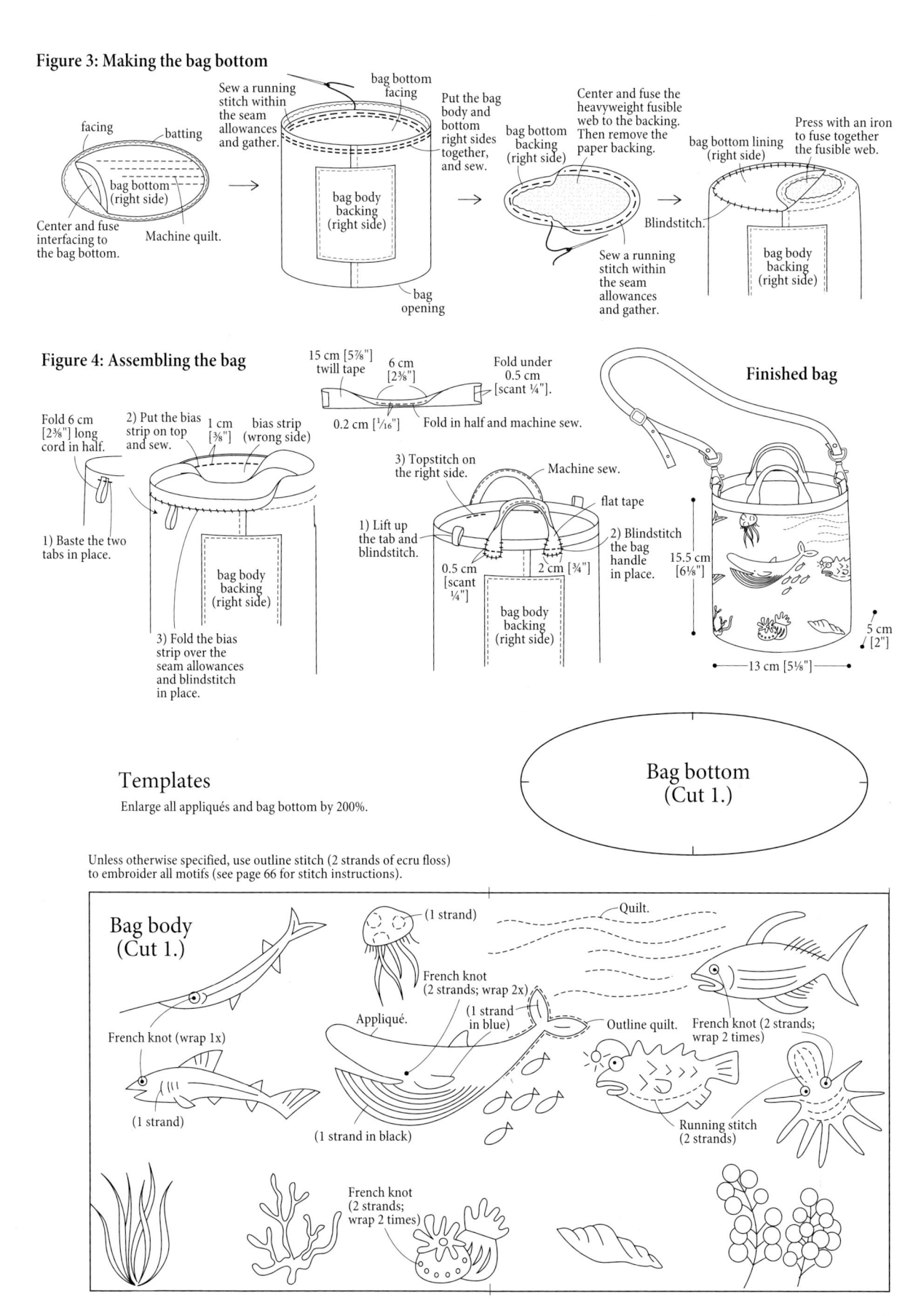

- facing
- batting
- bag bottom (right side)
- Center and fuse interfacing to the bag bottom.
- Machine quilt.

- Sew a running stitch within the seam allowances and gather.
- bag bottom facing
- Put the bag body and bottom right sides together, and sew.
- bag body backing (right side)
- bag opening

- Center and fuse the heavyweight fusible web to the backing. Then remove the paper backing.
- bag bottom backing (right side)
- Blindstitch.
- Sew a running stitch within the seam allowances and gather.

- Press with an iron to fuse together the fusible web.
- bag bottom lining (right side)
- bag body backing (right side)

Figure 4: Assembling the bag

- Fold 6 cm [2⅜"] long cord in half.
- 1) Baste the two tabs in place.
- 2) Put the bias strip on top and sew.
- 1 cm [⅜"]
- bias strip (wrong side)
- bag body backing (right side)
- 3) Fold the bias strip over the seam allowances and blindstitch in place.

- 15 cm [5⅞"] twill tape
- 6 cm [2⅜"]
- Fold under 0.5 cm [scant ¼"].
- 0.2 cm [1/16"]
- Fold in half and machine sew.

- 3) Topstitch on the right side.
- Machine sew.
- 1) Lift up the tab and blindstitch.
- flat tape
- 2) Blindstitch the bag handle in place.
- 0.5 cm [scant ¼"]
- 2 cm [¾"]
- bag body backing (right side)

Finished bag
- 15.5 cm [6⅛"]
- 5 cm [2"]
- 13 cm [5⅛"]

Templates

Enlarge all appliqués and bag bottom by 200%.

Bag bottom (Cut 1.)

Unless otherwise specified, use outline stitch (2 strands of ecru floss) to embroider all motifs (see page 66 for stitch instructions).

Bag body (Cut 1.)

- French knot (wrap 1x)
- (1 strand)
- (1 strand)
- Appliqué.
- French knot (2 strands; wrap 2x)
- (1 strand in blue)
- (1 strand in black)
- Quilt.
- Outline quilt.
- French knot (2 strands; wrap 2 times)
- Running stitch (2 strands)
- French knot (2 strands; wrap 2 times)

22

Project page 40
Templates on page 103

Tissue Holder

Materials Needed

Cottons:
- Stripe for tissue holder body: 20 x 50 cm [8" x 20"]
- Polka dot for lid: 20 x 20 cm [8" x 8"]
- Assorted fat quarters and scraps for appliqués
- Backing: 20 x 70 cm [8" x 28"]
- Bias-cut binding in two different prints or wovens: 3.5 x 45 cm [1⅜" x 18"] each

Batting: 20 x 70 cm [8" x 28"]
Heavyweight fusible interfacing: 15 x 15 cm [6" x 6"]
Grommet (inner diameter: 2.6 cm [1"])
Embroidery floss in various colors

Instructions

1 Referring to the diagram opposite top and the templates on page 103, stitch appliqués and embroideries on the tissue holder body top.

2 Layer the piece prepared in step 1 with batting and backing. Quilt as desired.

3 Layer the tissue holder lid top with batting and backing fused with heavyweight interfacing. Quilt. Cut out a circle from the center for the grommet. Machine sew along the edge (figure 1).

4 Sew the side edges of the quilted tissue holder body together to make a loop. Bind the seam allowances with the excess batting (figure 2).

5 Bind the bottom edge of the tissue holder body (figure 3).

6 Sew the lid to the upper edge of the tissue body holder with backing sides together. Bind the outer edge (figure 4). Install the grommet in the lid.

Tissue holder lid: Cut 1 for top, batting, heavyweight interfacing, and backing.

Do not add seam allowances when cutting interfacing. Cut all other pieces with 0.7 cm [¼"] seam allowances.

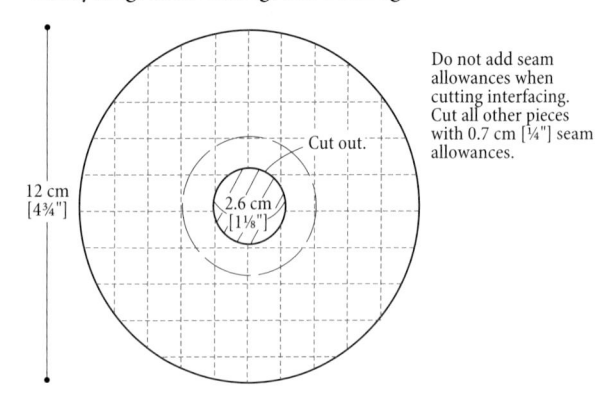

12 cm [4¾"]
2.6 cm [1⅛"]
Cut out.

Figure 1: Preparing the lid

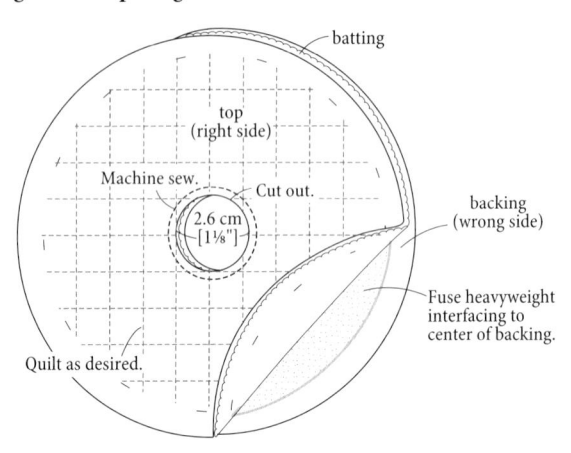

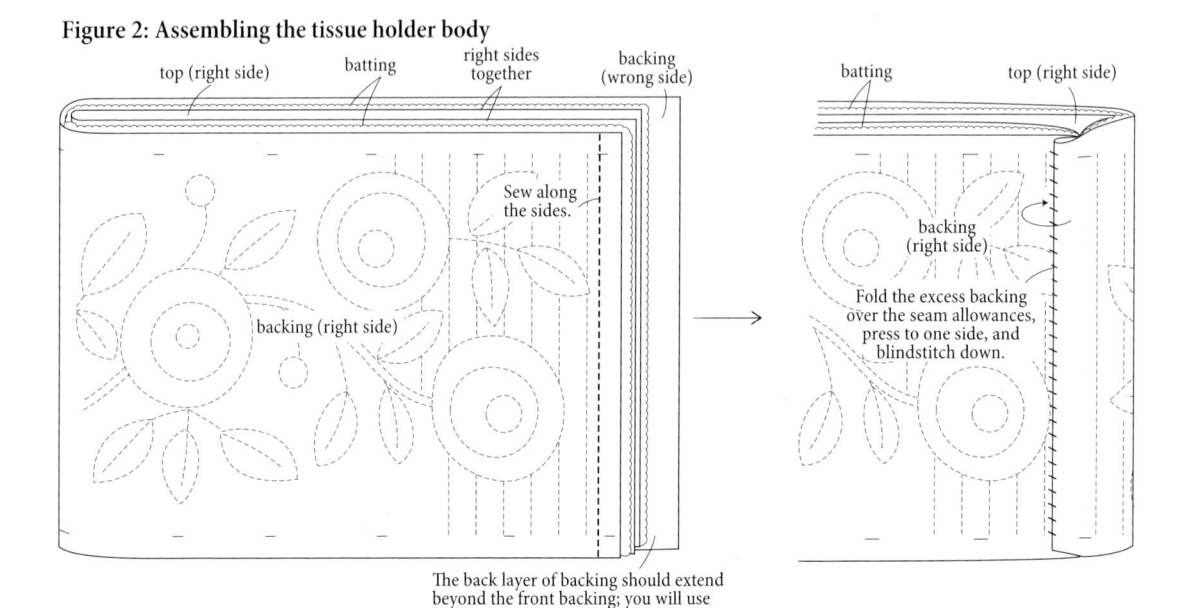

batting
top (right side)
Machine sew.
Cut out.
2.6 cm [1⅛"]
backing (wrong side)
Fuse heavyweight interfacing to center of backing.
Quilt as desired.

Figure 2: Assembling the tissue holder body

top (right side)
batting
right sides together
backing (wrong side)
Sew along the sides.
backing (right side)

The back layer of backing should extend beyond the front backing; you will use this excess to bind the seam allowances.

batting
top (right side)
backing (right side)
Fold the excess backing over the seam allowances, press to one side, and blindstitch down.

Tissue holder body: Cut 1 for top, batting, and backing.

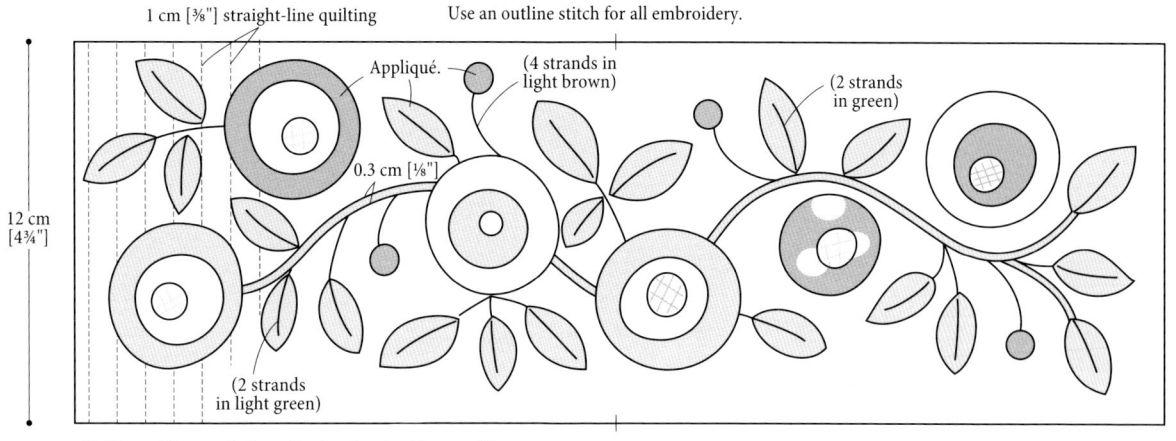

- 1 cm [3/8"] straight-line quilting
- Use an outline stitch for all embroidery.
- Appliqué.
- (4 strands in light brown)
- (2 strands in green)
- 0.3 cm [1/8"]
- (2 strands in light green)
- 12 cm [4¾"]
- 38 cm [15"]
- Outline quilt around all appliqué and embroidery motifs.

- When cutting appliqués, add 0.3 to 0.4 cm [1/8"] seam allowances. When cutting backing, add 1.5 cm [5/8"] seam allowances to the right side edge only. Cut all other edges and pieces with 0.7 cm [1/4"] seam allowances.
- Stitch appliqués and embroidery designs on the tissue holder body top.
- Make a quilt sandwich with top, batting, and backing; machine quilt.

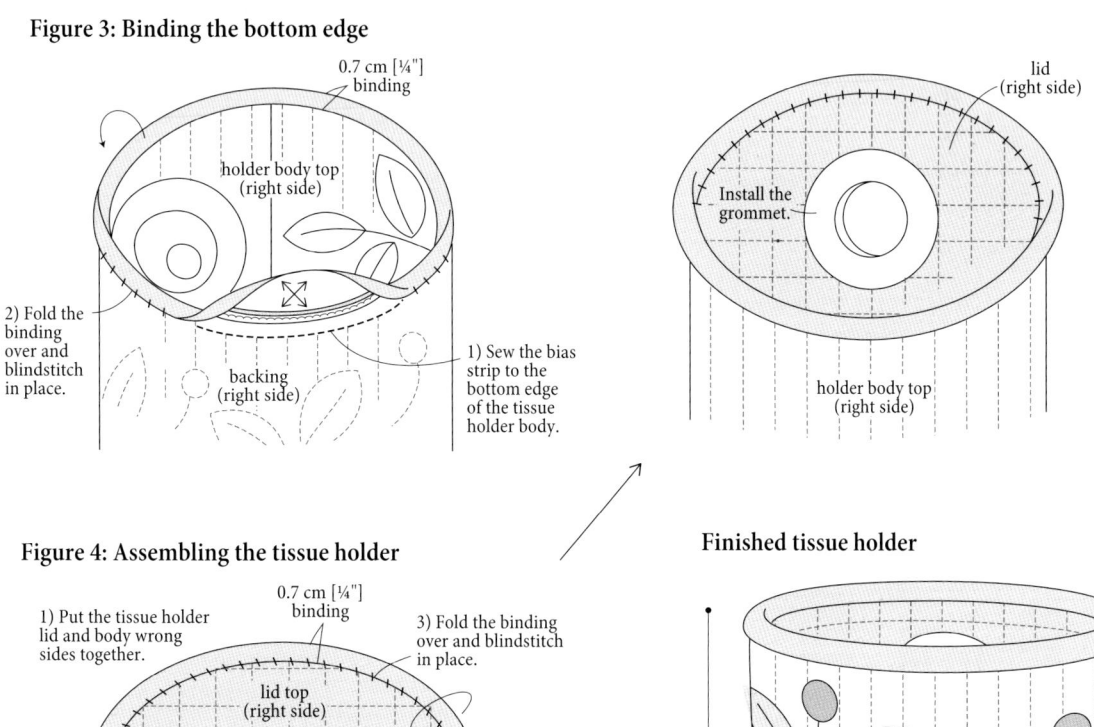

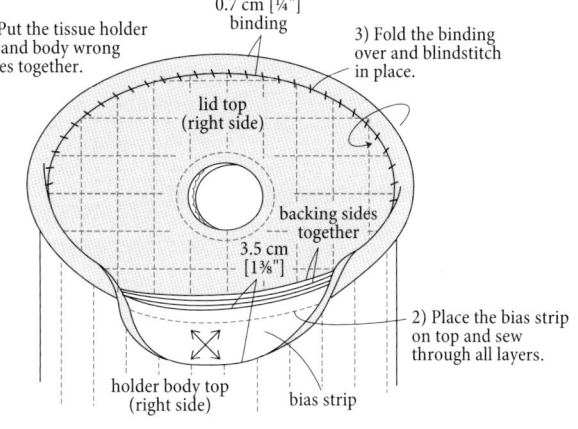

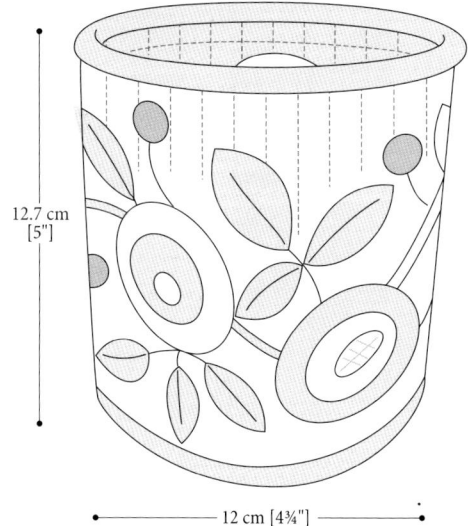

Figure 3: Binding the bottom edge

- 0.7 cm [1/4"] binding
- holder body top (right side)
- 2) Fold the binding over and blindstitch in place.
- 1) Sew the bias strip to the bottom edge of the tissue holder body.
- backing (right side)

- lid (right side)
- Install the grommet.
- holder body top (right side)

Figure 4: Assembling the tissue holder

- 1) Put the tissue holder lid and body wrong sides together.
- 0.7 cm [1/4"] binding
- 3) Fold the binding over and blindstitch in place.
- lid top (right side)
- backing sides together
- 3.5 cm [1 3/8"]
- 2) Place the bias strip on top and sew through all layers.
- holder body top (right side)
- bias strip

Finished tissue holder

- 12.7 cm [5"]
- 12 cm [4¾"]

23

Project page 41
Full-size templates on page 93

Glasses Case

Materials Needed

Cottons:
- Gingham for case front and back: 25 x 20 cm [10" x 8"]
- Assorted fat quarters and scraps for appliqués and tab
- Backing: 30 x 25 cm [12" x 10"]
- Bias-cut binding: 2.5 x 35 cm [1" x 14"]

Batting: 30 x 25 cm [12" x 10"]
15 cm [6"] zipper
Embroidery floss in various colors

Instructions

1 Referring to the diagram above right and the full-size templates on page 93, stitch appliqués and embroideries on the gingham case front top.

2 Layer the case front top with batting and backing. Sew along the top edge, then turn right side out. Quilt as desired. Sew one edge of the zipper tape to the top edge (figure 1). Repeat with the case front back.

Case front/back: Cut 2 pieces each for the top, batting, and backing.

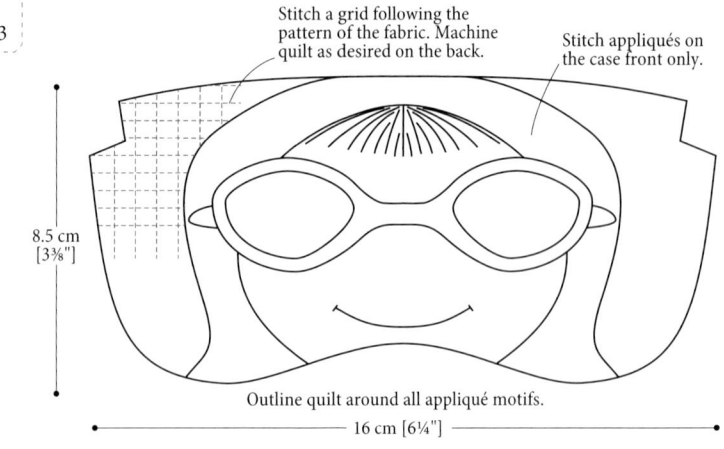

Stitch a grid following the pattern of the fabric. Machine quilt as desired on the back.

Stitch appliqués on the case front only.

8.5 cm [3⅜"]

Outline quilt around all appliqué motifs.

16 cm [6¼"]

Tab: Cut 1.

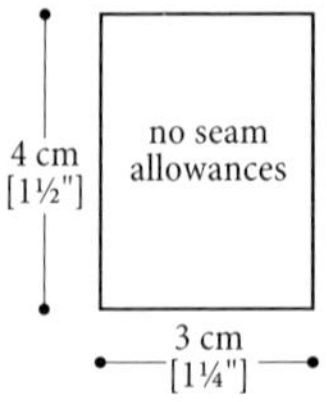

4 cm [1½"]
no seam allowances
3 cm [1¼"]

- When cutting appliqués, add 0.3 to 0.4 cm [⅛"] seam allowances. Cut all other pieces with 1 cm [⅜"] seam allowances.
- Stitch appliqués and embroidery designs on the case front top.

Figure 1: Quilting and assembling the case

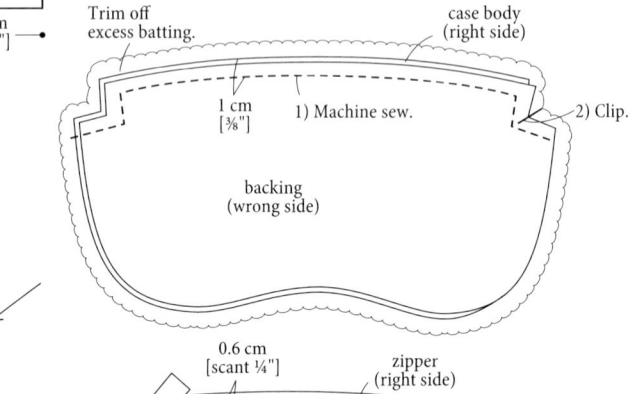

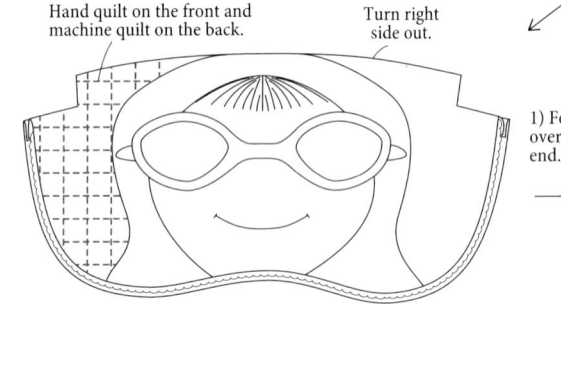

Trim off excess batting.
case body (right side)
1 cm [⅜"]
1) Machine sew.
2) Clip.
backing (wrong side)

Hand quilt on the front and machine quilt on the back.
Turn right side out.

0.6 cm [scant ¼"]
zipper (right side)
1) Fold over the end.
0.2 cm [1/16"]
2) Layer the case body and zipper, and machine sew.

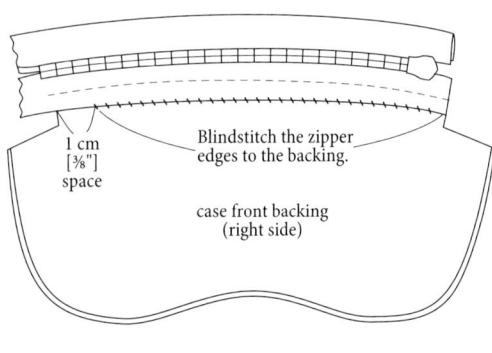

1 cm [⅜"] space
Blindstitch the zipper edges to the backing.
case front backing (right side)

Sew the case back and remaining edge of zipper in the same manner.

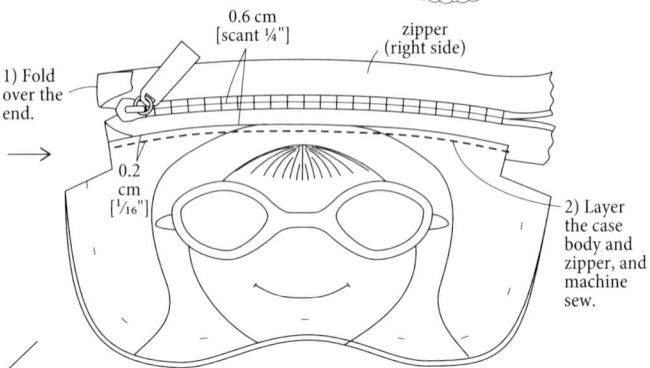

Figure 2: Joining the case front and back

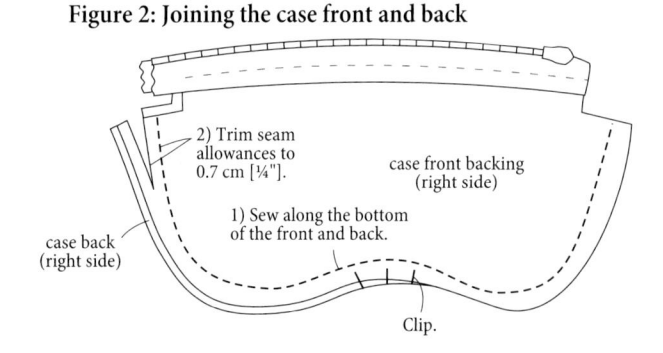

2) Trim seam allowances to 0.7 cm [¼"].
case front backing (right side)
1) Sew along the bottom of the front and back.
case back (right side)
Clip.

Figure 3: Binding the seams

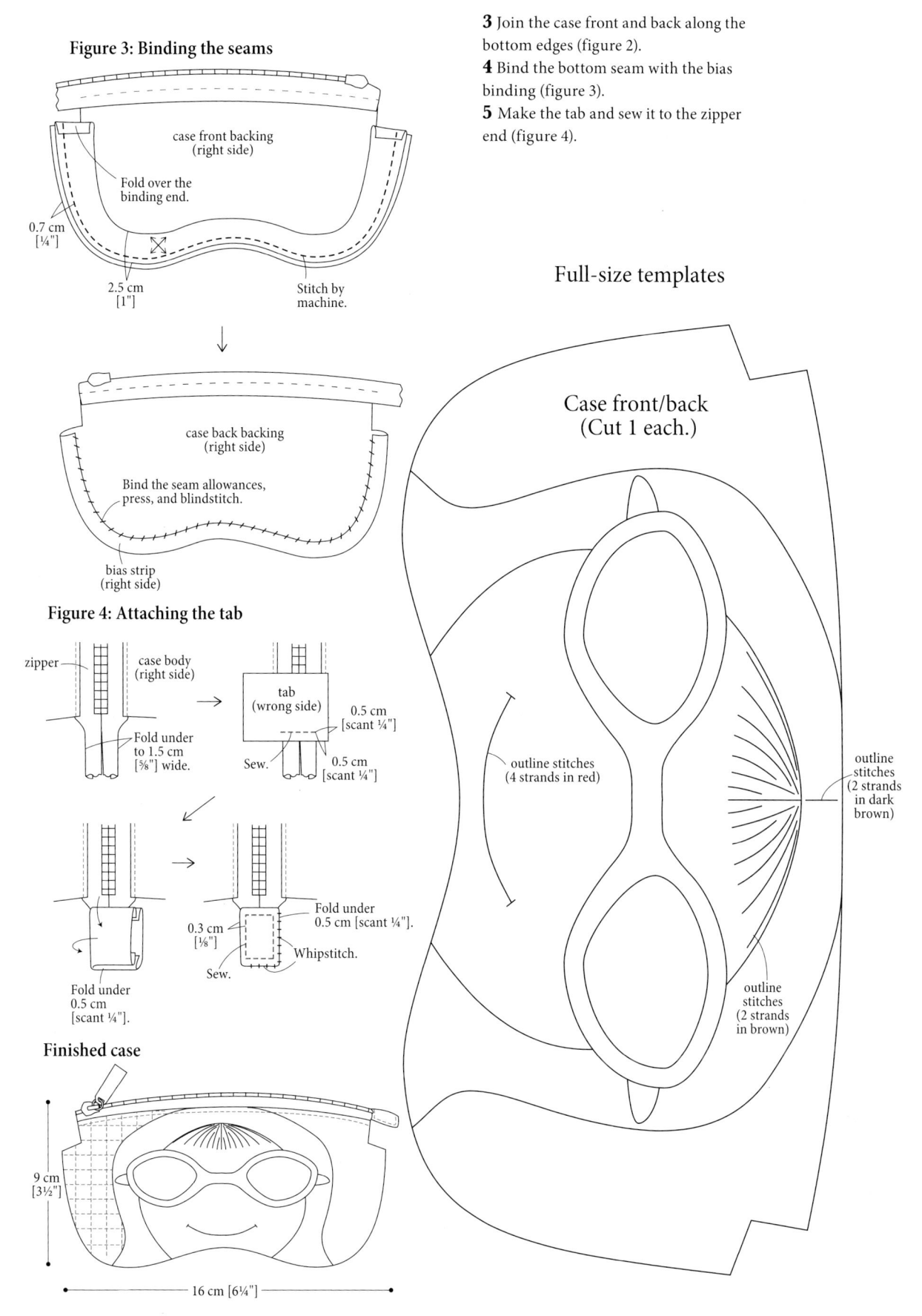

case front backing (right side)

Fold over the binding end.

0.7 cm [¼"]

2.5 cm [1"]

Stitch by machine.

case back backing (right side)

Bind the seam allowances, press, and blindstitch.

bias strip (right side)

Figure 4: Attaching the tab

zipper — case body (right side)

Fold under to 1.5 cm [⅝"] wide.

tab (wrong side)

0.5 cm [scant ¼"]

Sew.

0.5 cm [scant ¼"]

Fold under 0.5 cm [scant ¼"].

0.3 cm [⅛"]

Fold under 0.5 cm [scant ¼"].

Whipstitch.

Sew.

Finished case

9 cm [3½"]

16 cm [6¼"]

3 Join the case front and back along the bottom edges (figure 2).
4 Bind the bottom seam with the bias binding (figure 3).
5 Make the tab and sew it to the zipper end (figure 4).

Full-size templates

Case front/back (Cut 1 each.)

outline stitches (4 strands in red)

outline stitches (2 strands in dark brown)

outline stitches (2 strands in brown)

93

24 Mobile Phone Case

Project page 42
Full-size templates on page 95

Materials Needed

Cottons:
- Stripe for case front background and shoulder strap: 25 x 120 cm [10" x 48"]
- Assorted scraps for appliqués
- Backing: 50 x 35 cm [20" x 14"]
- Polka dot for gusset and case back: 45 x 25 cm [18" x 10"]

Batting: 50 x 35 cm [20" x 14"]
Embroidery floss in white
1 pair metal purse clasps (12 x 6 cm [4¾" x 2⅜"])

Instructions

1 Referring the diagrams above right and the full-size templates on page 95, stitch appliqués and embroideries on the case front top.

Case front: Cut 1 each from top, batting, and backing.
- Quilt following the pattern of the fabric.
- Leave open 8 cm [3⅛"].
- Appliqué.
- gusset position
- 19 cm [7½"]
- colonial knot (6 strands in white)
- Outline quilt around all appliqué motifs.
- 13 cm [5⅛"]

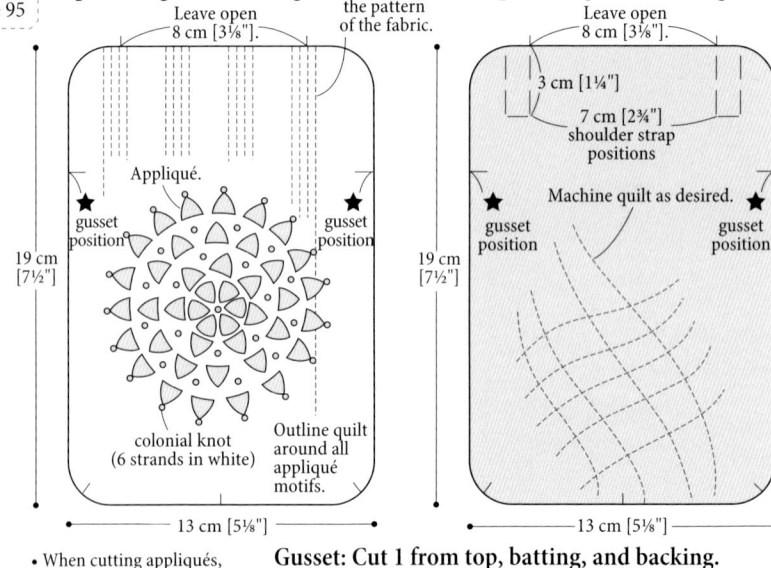

Case back: Cut 1 each from top, batting, and backing.
- Leave open 8 cm [3⅛"].
- 3 cm [1¼"]
- 7 cm [2¾"] shoulder strap positions
- gusset position
- Machine quilt as desired.
- 19 cm [7½"]
- 13 cm [5⅛"]

- When cutting appliqués, add 0.3 to 0.4 cm [⅛"] seam allowances. Cut all other pieces with 0.7 cm [¼"] seam allowances.
- Stitch appliqués and embroidery designs on the case front top.

Gusset: Cut 1 from top, batting, and backing.
- Leave open 8 cm [3⅛"].
- Machine quilt.
- 2 cm [¾"]
- on fold
- 38.6 cm [15¼"]

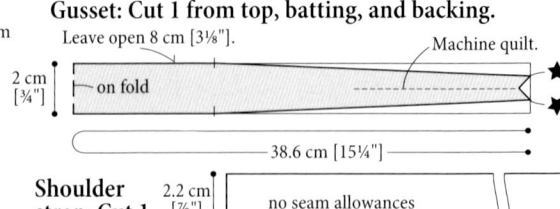

Shoulder strap: Cut 1.
- 2.2 cm [⅞"]
- no seam allowances
- 115 cm [45¼"]

Figure 1: Assembling the case front

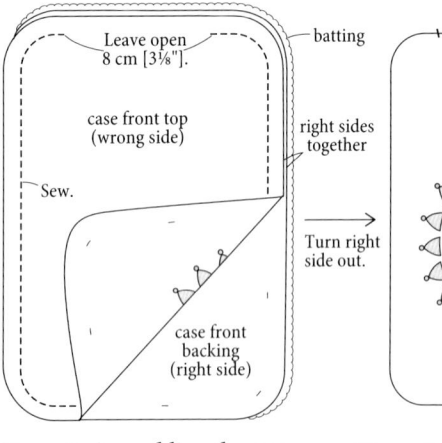

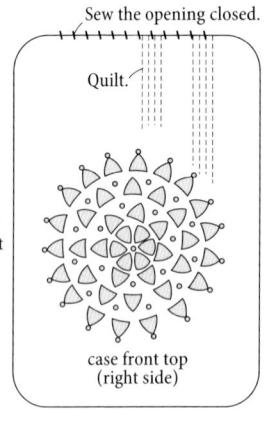

- Leave open 8 cm [3⅛"].
- batting
- case front top (wrong side)
- right sides together
- Sew.
- case front backing (right side)
- Turn right side out.
- Sew the opening closed.
- Quilt.
- case front top (right side)

Figure 4: Making and adding the shoulder strap

- Fold in fourths.
- 0.2 cm [1/16"]
- 1.1 cm [½"]
- on fold
- Edgestitch by machine.
- Fold under the end.
- 1.5 cm [⅝"]
- 3 cm [1¼"]
- 7 cm [2¾"]
- case back top (right side)
- Sew to secure.

Make the case back and gusset in the same manner.

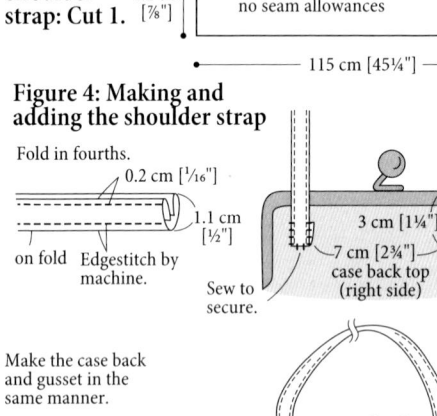

Figure 2: Assembling the case

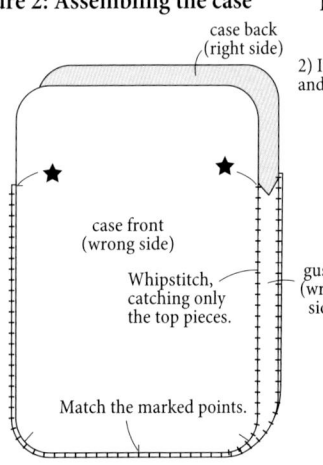

- case back (right side)
- case front (wrong side)
- Whipstitch, catching only the top pieces.
- gusset (wrong side)
- Match the marked points.

Figure 3: Attaching the metal clasps

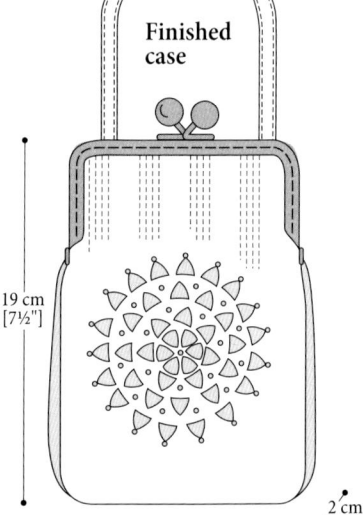

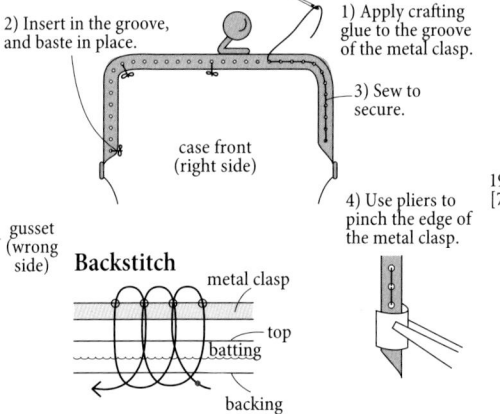

1) Apply crafting glue to the groove of the metal clasp.
2) Insert in the groove, and baste in place.
3) Sew to secure.
4) Use pliers to pinch the edge of the metal clasp.

case front (right side)

Backstitch
- metal clasp
- top
- batting
- backing

Finished case
- 19 cm [7½"]
- 13 cm [5⅛"]
- 2 cm [¾"]

2 Put the piece prepared in step 1 with backing and batting right sides together; sew all around, leaving an opening to turn right side out (figure 1).
3 Turn right side out and quilt. Sew the case back and gusset in the same manner.

4 Put the case front, back, and gusset right sides together. Whipstitch edges together to make case body (figure 2).

5 Attach the metal clasps (figure 3).
6 Make a shoulder strap and sew to the case back (figure 4).

Colonial knot

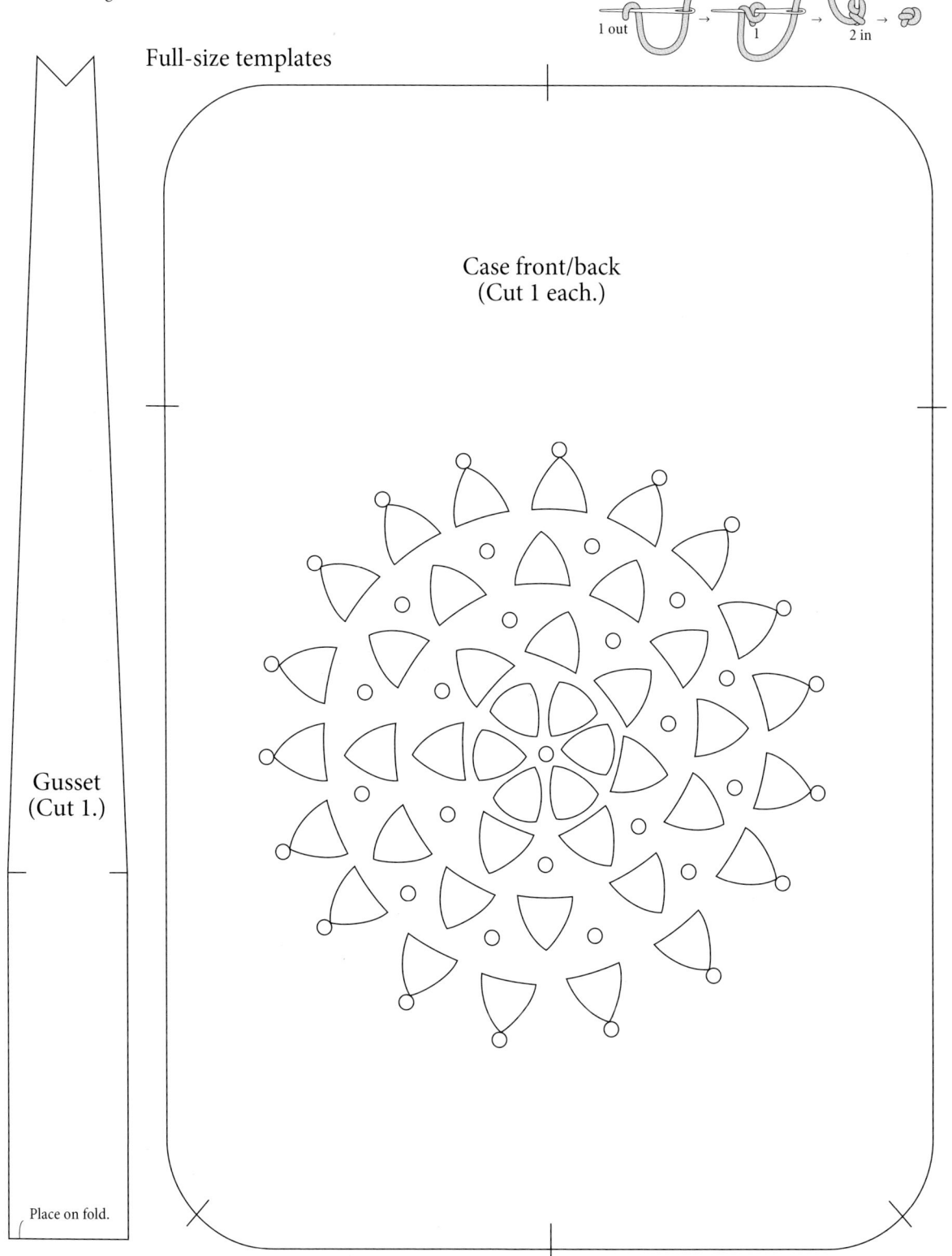

1 out → 1 → 2 in

Full-size templates

Case front/back
(Cut 1 each.)

Gusset
(Cut 1.)

Place on fold.

95

25

Project page 44 Full-size templates on page 103

Water Bottle Carrier

Materials Needed

Cottons:
- Brown print for carrier front and back: 30 x 25 cm [12" x 10"]
- Assorted fat quarters and scraps for appliqués and facing to cover handle ends
- Light yarn-dye for one gusset: 20 x 15 cm [8" x 6"]
- Print for one gusset: 20 x 15 cm [8" x 6"]
- Print for carrier bottom: 15 x 15 cm [6" x 6"]
- Handle: 25 x 10 cm [10" x 4"]
- Backing: 55 x 25 cm [22" x 10"]
- Bias binding: 3.5 x 60 cm [1⅜" x 24"]

Batting: 50 x 20 cm [20" x 8"]
Fusible interfacing: 2 x 20 cm [¾" x 8"]

Instructions

1 Referring to the diagrams at right and the full-size templates on page 103, stitch appliqués on the patchwork pieces for the carrier front and back. Piece patches to make the carrier top; layer with batting and facing. Quilt as desired.

Handle: Cut 1 for top and interfacing.

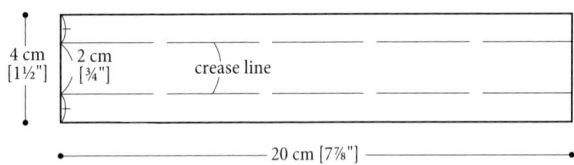

- Refer to diagram below to add seam allowances when cutting the handle top fabric. Refer to diagram below to cut interfacing.
- Center and fuse interfacing to the handle.

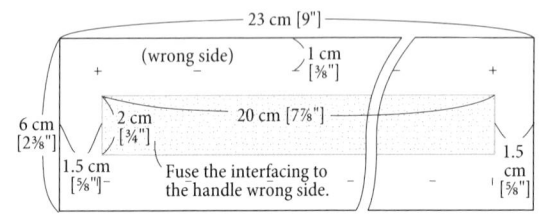

Figure 1: Making the handle

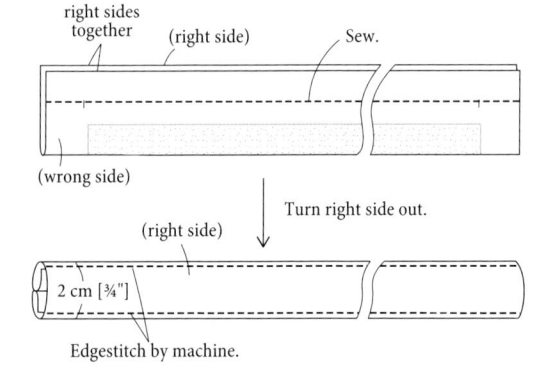

Carrier body: Cut 1 for top, batting, and backing.

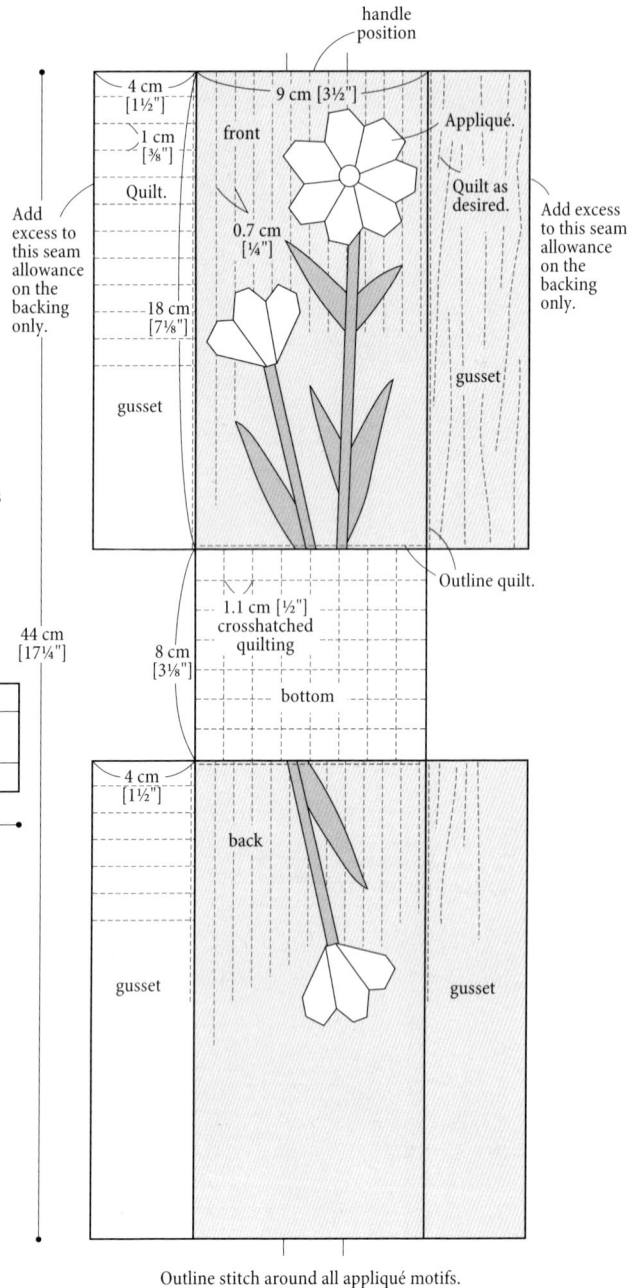

- Cut patchwork pieces for gusset, front, back, and bottom from desired fabrics, adding 0.7 cm [¼"] seam allowances. When cutting appliqués, add 0.3 to 0.4 cm [⅛"] seam allowances.
- Cut the facing, lining, and batting the size of the entire top piece, adding 1 cm [⅜"] seam allowances; on the two indicated gusset edges, cut the side seam allowances of the backing at 2 cm [¾"] instead.
- Stitch appliqués on the front and back patchwork pieces.
- Piece together the gusset, front, back, and bottom rectangles to make the carrier top.
- Make a quilt sandwich with top, batting, and backing; quilt.

2 Make the handle (figure 1).

3 Bind the carrier openings using the bias binding strip. Sew along the side edges and bind with the excess backing fabric (figure 2).

4 To make the gussets, fold the carrier so the bottom and side edges align at the bottom corner openings. Sew across each corner edge (figure 3).

5 Attach the handle to the carrier body and cover with a facing (figure 4).

Figure 2: Assembling the carrier body

1) Bind the opening edges of the quilted carrier body.

0.7 cm [¼"] binding

0.7 cm [¼"]

front top (right side)

back top (right side)

batting

backing (right side)

batting

right sides together

backing (wrong side)

2) Fold the front/back piece in half right sides together, and sew along both side edges.

The back layer of backing should extend beyond the front backing; you will use this excess to bind the seam allowances.

center of the carrier bottom on fold

Blindstitch.

0.7 cm [¼"] binding

Fold the excess backing over the seam allowances, and blindstitch in place.

backing (right side)

center of the carrier bottom on fold

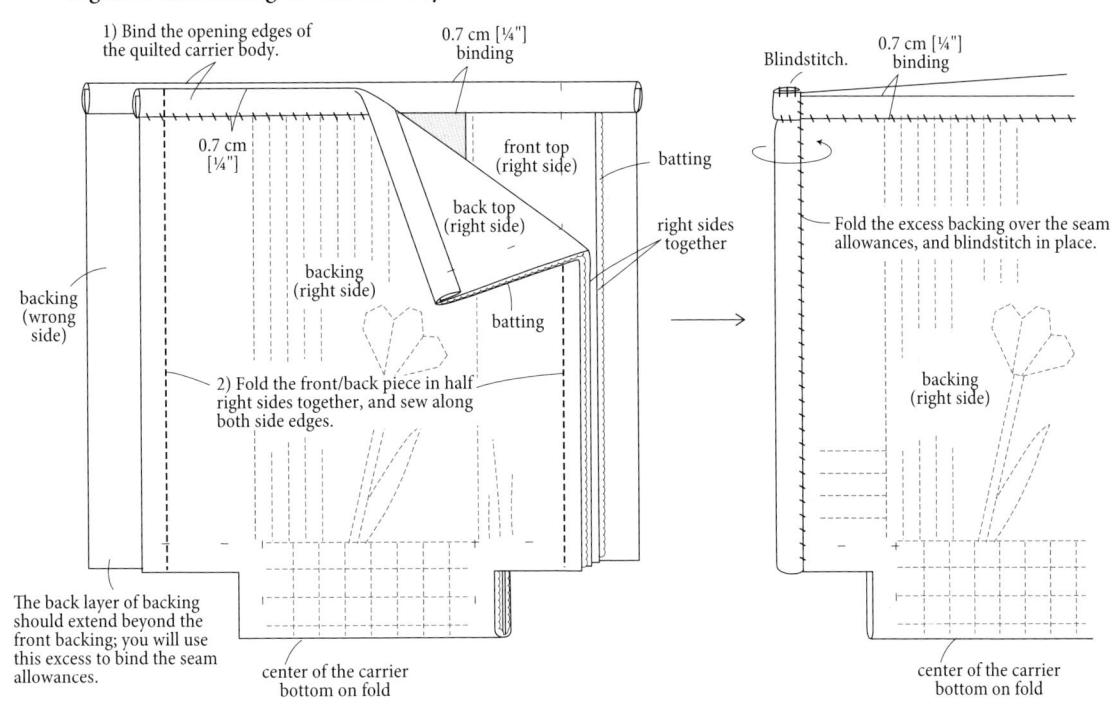

Figure 3: Making the gusset

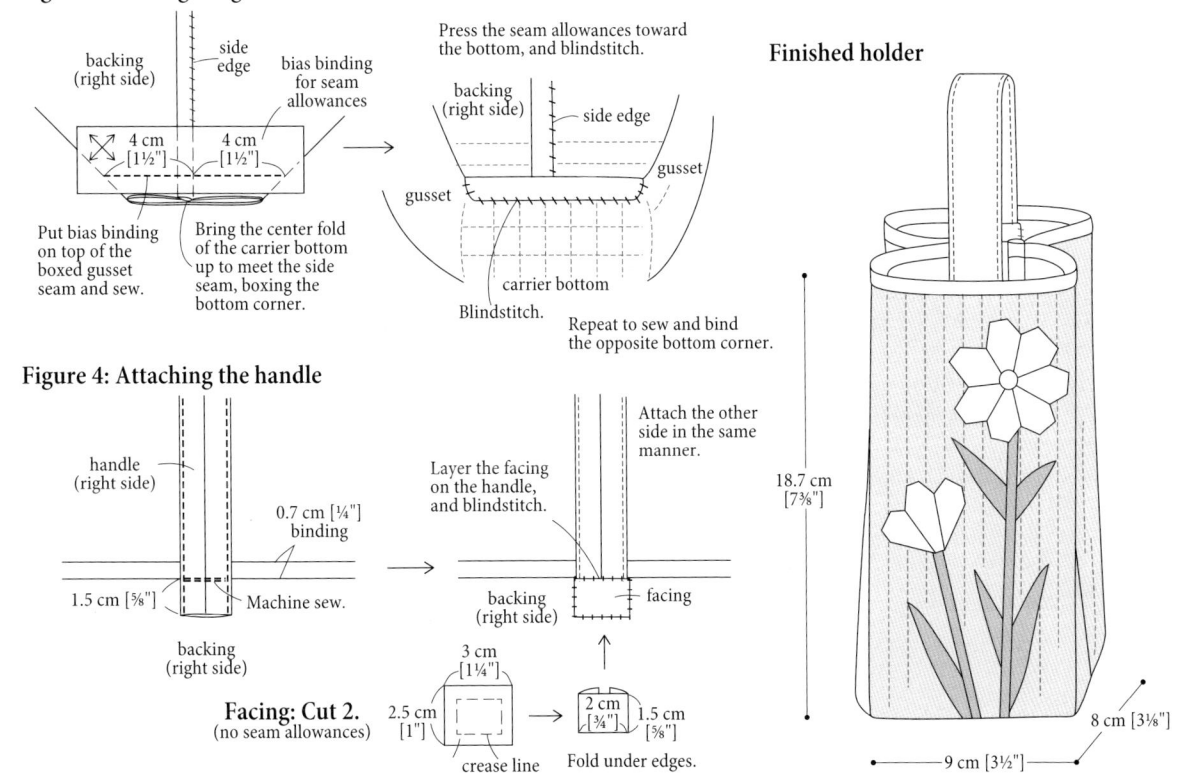

backing (right side)

side edge

bias binding for seam allowances

4 cm [1½"]   4 cm [1½"]

Put bias binding on top of the boxed gusset seam and sew.

Bring the center fold of the carrier bottom up to meet the side seam, boxing the bottom corner.

Press the seam allowances toward the bottom, and blindstitch.

backing (right side)

side edge

gusset

gusset

carrier bottom

Blindstitch.

Repeat to sew and bind the opposite bottom corner.

Figure 4: Attaching the handle

handle (right side)

0.7 cm [¼"] binding

1.5 cm [⅝"] — Machine sew.

backing (right side)

Facing: Cut 2.
(no seam allowances)

2.5 cm [1"]

3 cm [1¼"]

crease line

2 cm [¾"]   1.5 cm [⅝"]

Fold under edges.

Layer the facing on the handle, and blindstitch.

Attach the other side in the same manner.

backing (right side)

facing

Finished holder

18.7 cm [7⅜"]

9 cm [3½"]

8 cm [3⅛"]

26 Card Case

Project page 46

Materials Needed

Cottons:
- Polka dot for card case top: 30 x 15 cm [12" x 6"]
- Assorted scraps for appliqué
- Backing: 30 x 20 cm [12" x 8"]

Batting: 30 x 20 cm [12" x 8"]
20 cm [8"] zipper; shorten to fit (7⅞")

Instructions

1 Stitch appliqués on the polka dot to make the case body top.
2 Layer the top prepared in step 1 with batting and backing; turn right side out. Quilt as desired.
3 Insert the zipper.
4 Machine sew the case bottom. Fold the excess backing over the seam allowances; blindstitch in place.

Full-size templates

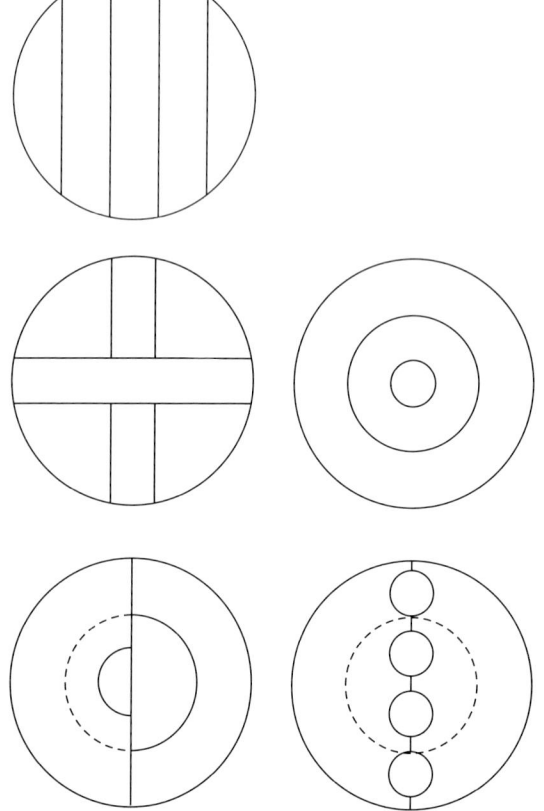

Card case: Cut 1 for top, batting, and backing.

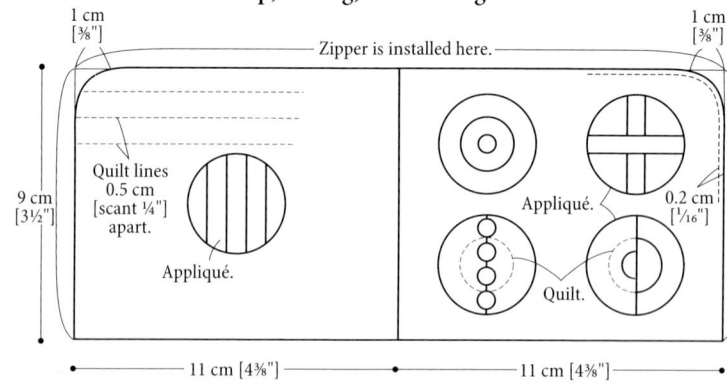

- When cutting appliqués, add 0.3 to 0.4 cm [⅛"] seam allowances. When cutting backing, add 1.5 cm [⅝"] seam allowances. Cut all other pieces with 1 cm [⅜"] seam allowances.
- Stitch appliqués and embroidery designs on the card case top.

Assembling the card case

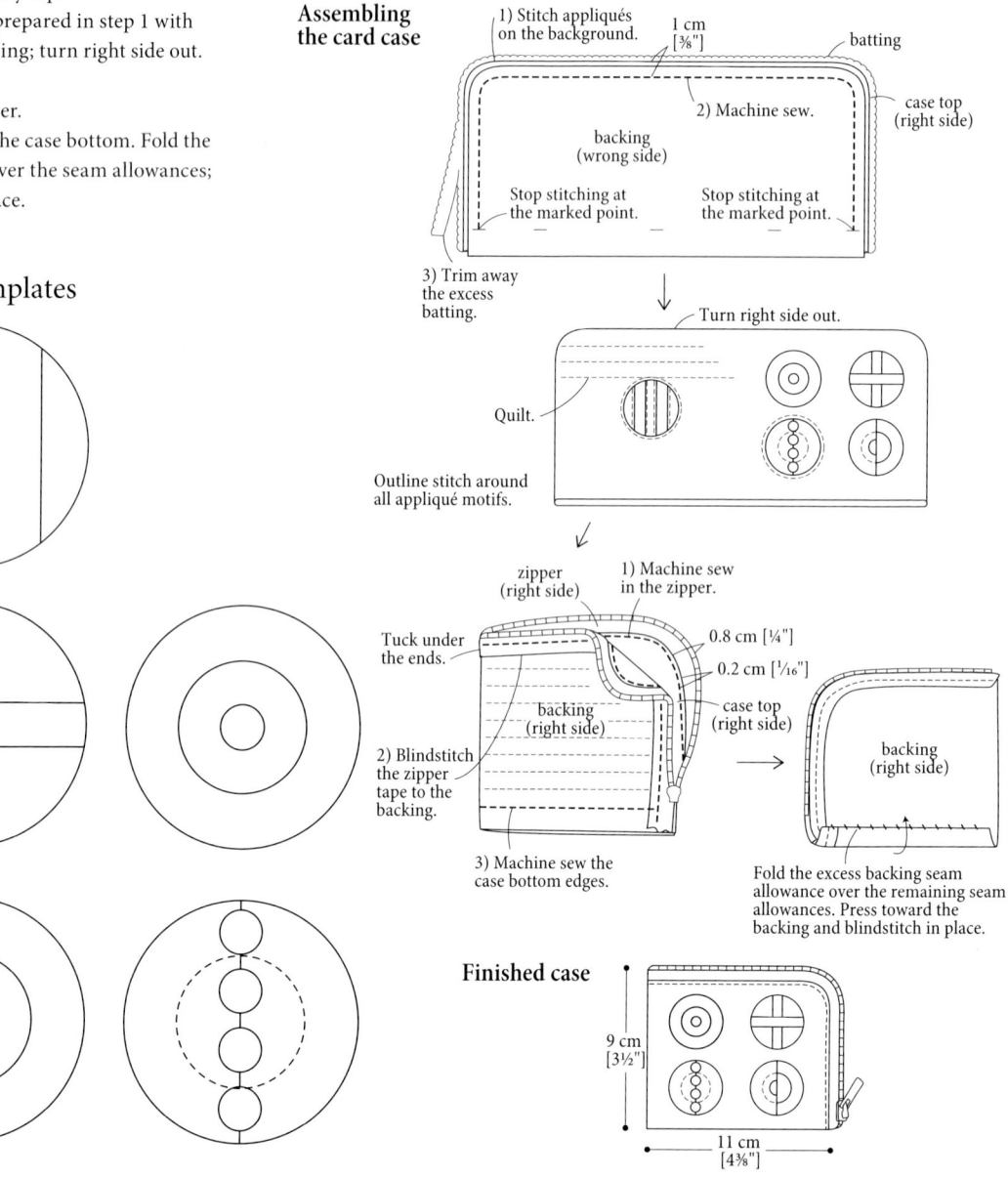

1) Stitch appliqués on the background.
2) Machine sew.
3) Trim away the excess batting.

Turn right side out.

Outline stitch around all appliqué motifs.

1) Machine sew in the zipper.
2) Blindstitch the zipper tape to the backing.
3) Machine sew the case bottom edges.

Fold the excess backing seam allowance over the remaining seam allowances. Press toward the backing and blindstitch in place.

Finished case

9 cm [3½"] × 11 cm [4⅜"]

01 Mini Pouch

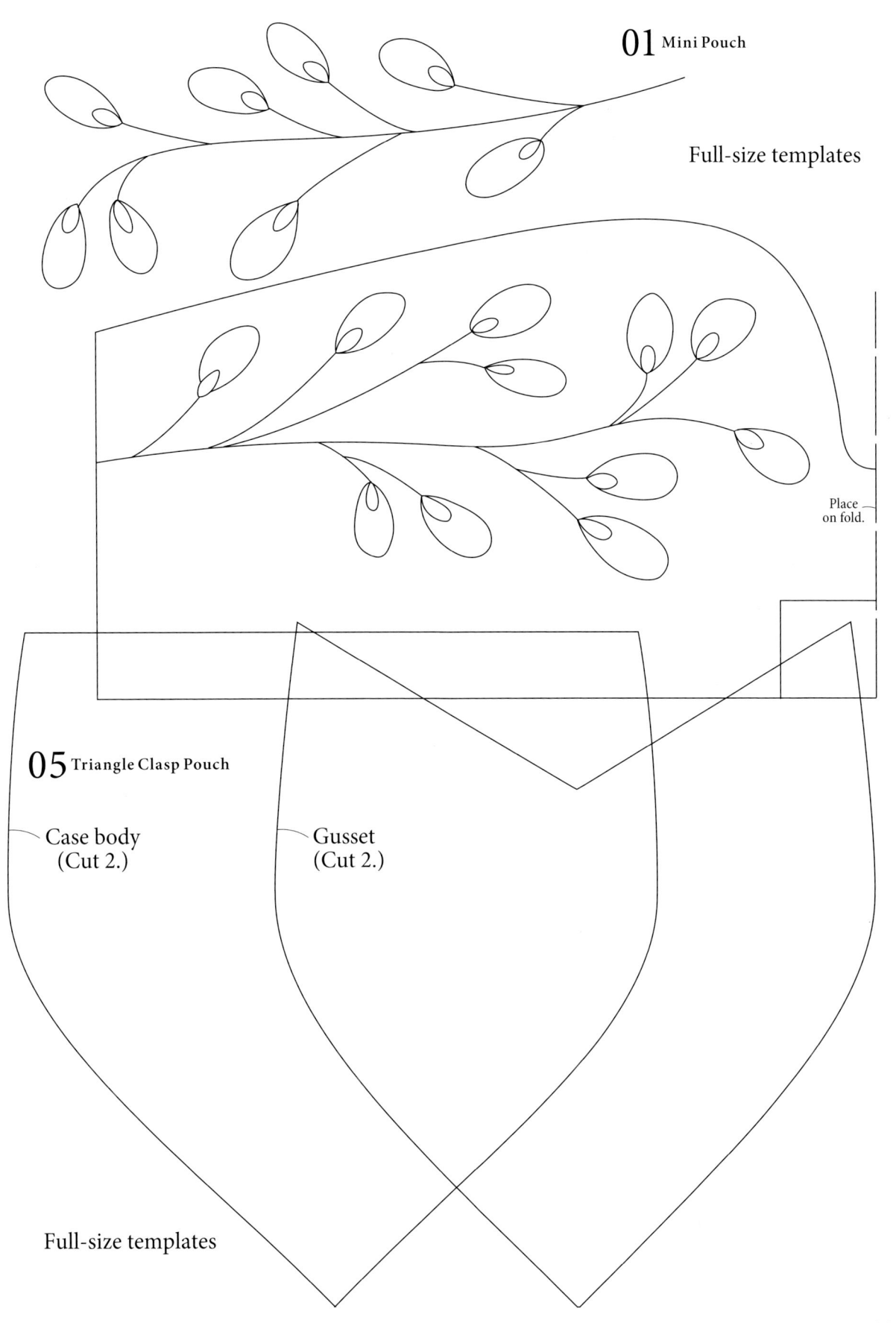

Full-size templates

Place on fold.

05 Triangle Clasp Pouch

Case body
(Cut 2.)

Gusset
(Cut 2.)

Full-size templates

99

02 Bluebird Pouch

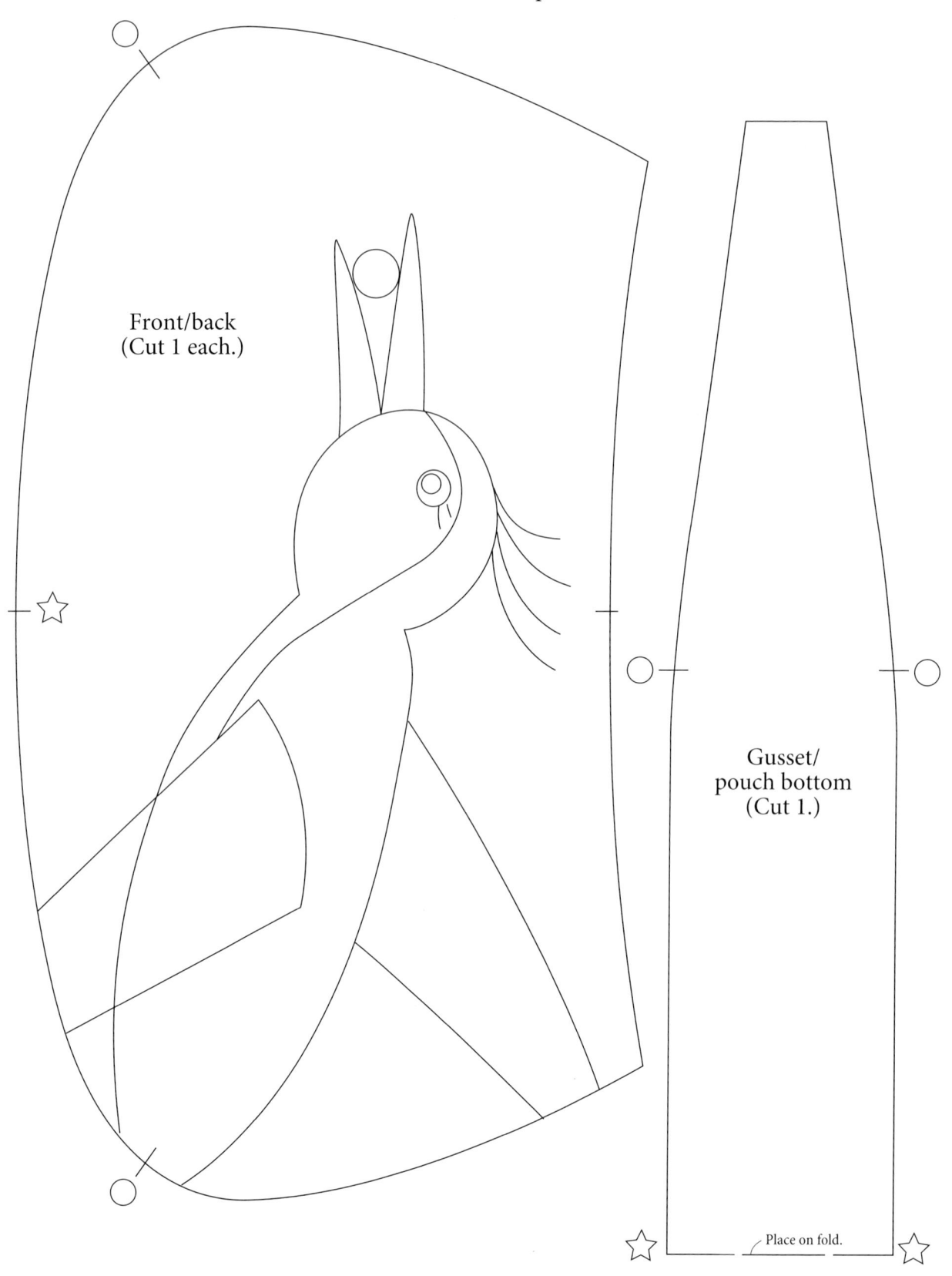

Full-size templates

Front/back
(Cut 1 each.)

Gusset/
pouch bottom
(Cut 1.)

Place on fold.

07 Tulip Pouch

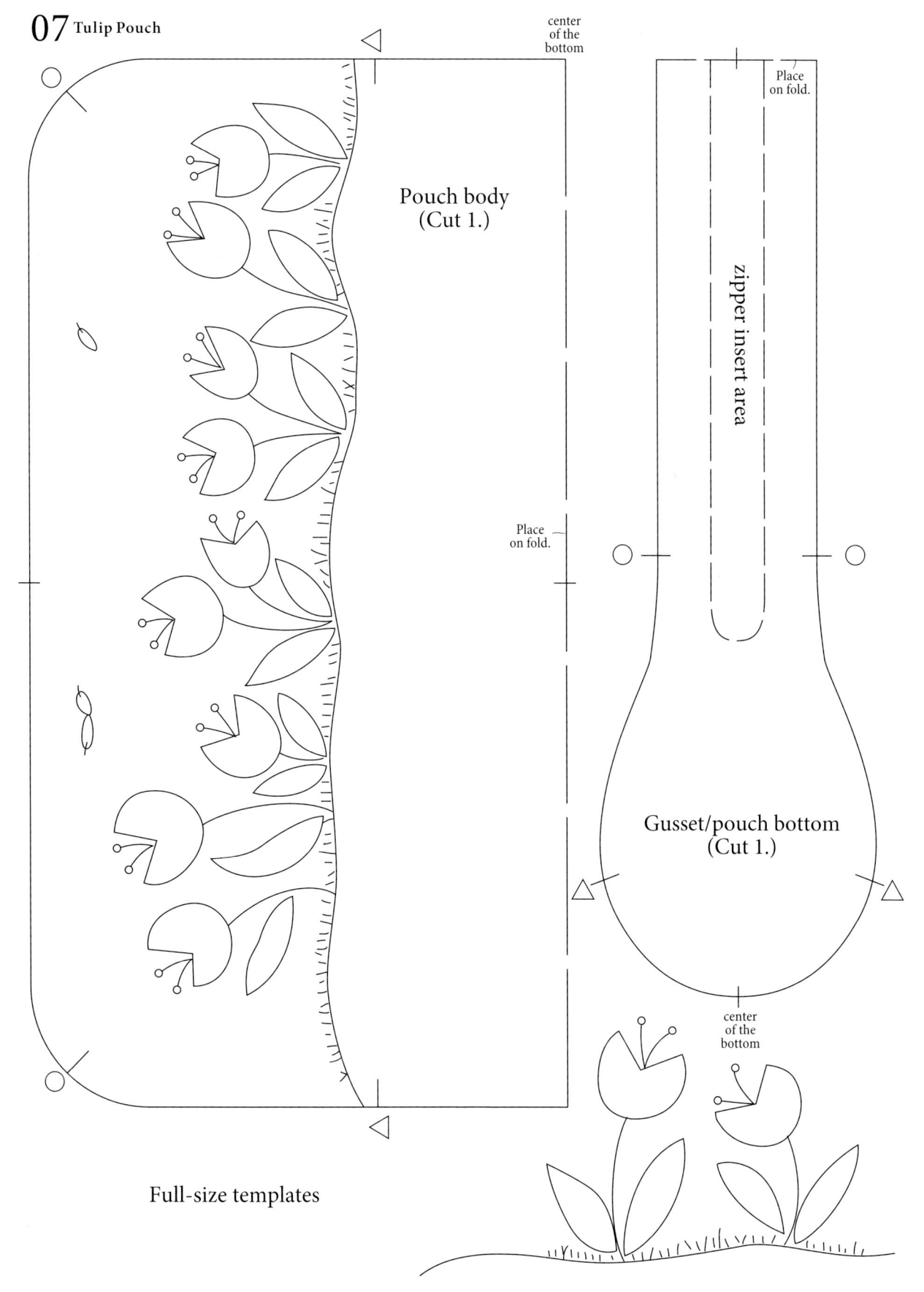

Pouch body (Cut 1.)

center of the bottom

Place on fold.

Place on fold.

zipper insert area

Gusset/pouch bottom (Cut 1.)

center of the bottom

Full-size templates

11, 12 Bunny Dolls

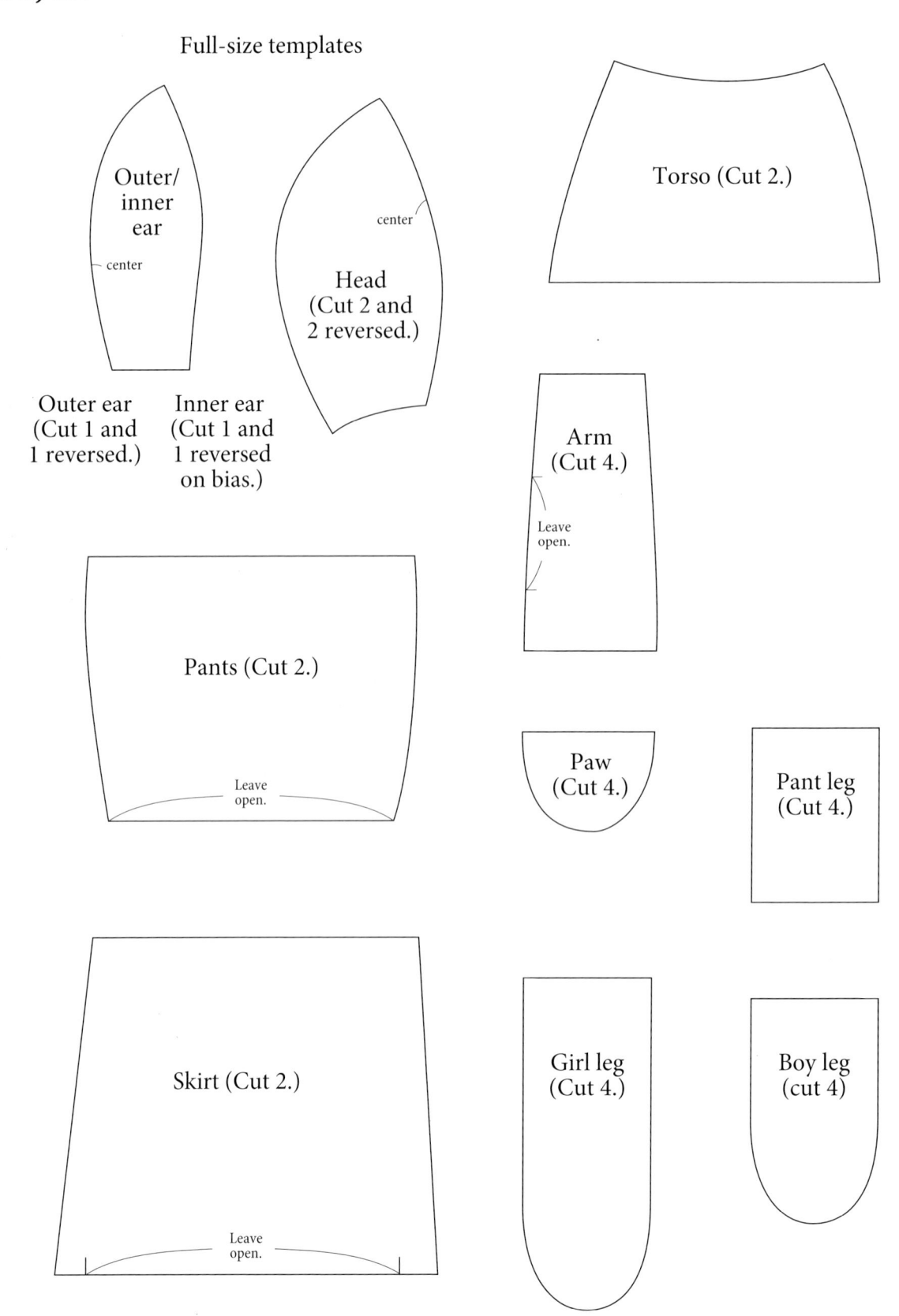

Full-size templates

Outer/inner ear
— center

Outer ear (Cut 1 and 1 reversed.)

Inner ear (Cut 1 and 1 reversed on bias.)

Head (Cut 2 and 2 reversed.)
center

Torso (Cut 2.)

Arm (Cut 4.)
Leave open.

Pants (Cut 2.)
Leave open.

Paw (Cut 4.)

Pant leg (Cut 4.)

Skirt (Cut 2.)
Leave open.

Girl leg (Cut 4.)

Boy leg (cut 4)

25 Water Bottle Carrier

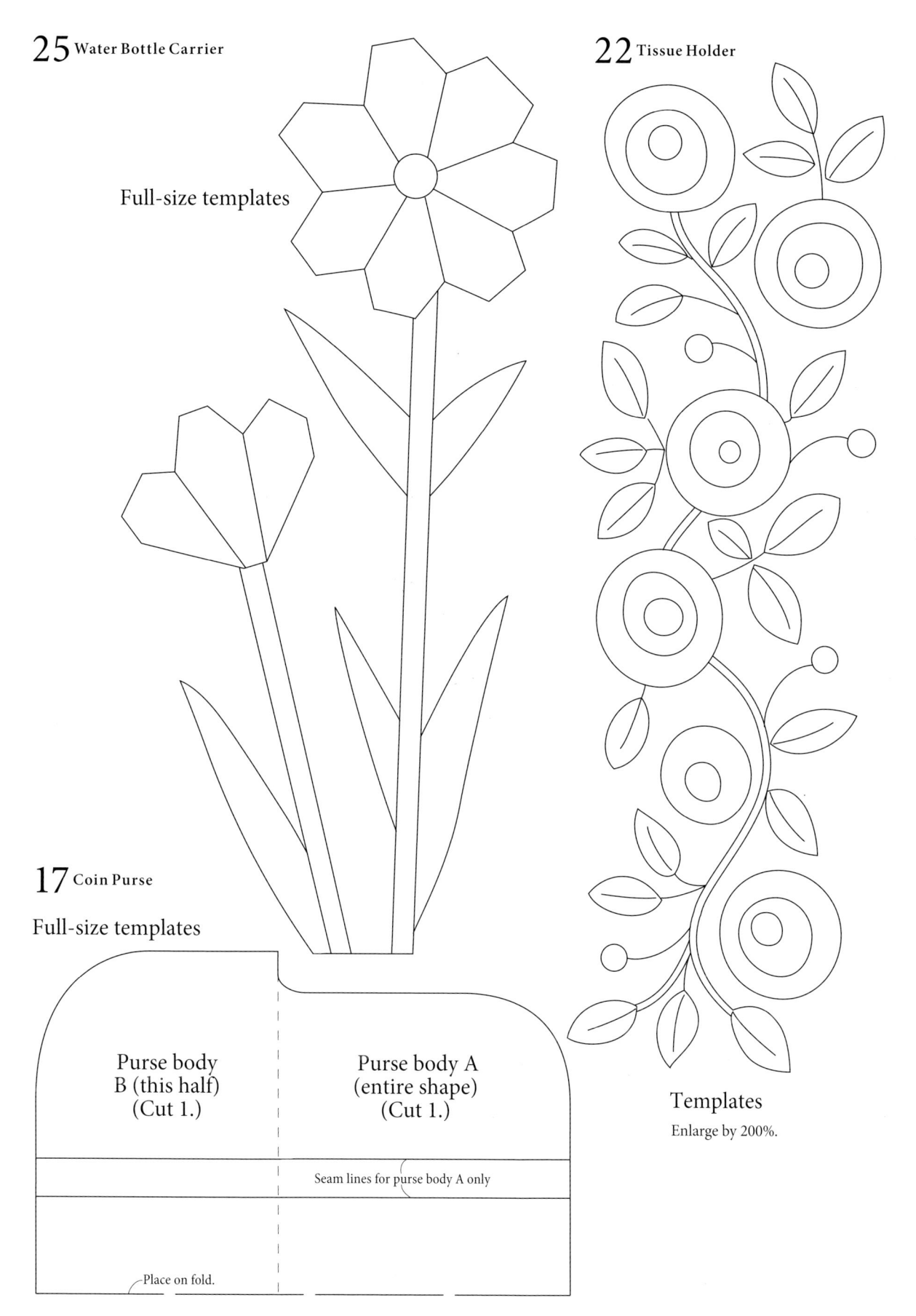

Full-size templates

22 Tissue Holder

17 Coin Purse

Full-size templates

Purse body B (this half) (Cut 1.)

Purse body A (entire shape) (Cut 1.)

Seam lines for purse body A only

Place on fold.

Templates

Enlarge by 200%.

Yoko Saito

Yoko Saito is from the prefecture of Chiba, Japan. She is popular not only in Japan but around the world, where fans love her unique use of color and meticulous needlework. She appears in a wide range of media including television and magazines. She heads Yoko Saito's Quilt School and shop, Quilt Party Co., Ltd., in Ichikawa City, about an hour northeast of Tokyo. She also instructs at Quilt-Juku (Nihon Vogue Corp.), NHK Culture Center, etc. She has authored a host of books, many of which have been translated into English and are published by Stitch Publications, LLC.

Quilt Party Co., Ltd.
Active Ichikawa 2-3F
1-23-2, Ichikawa, Ichikawa-shi,
Chiba-Ken, Japan 272-0034

http://www.quilt.co.jp (Japanese)

Original Title	Saito Yoko no Tenohira no Takaramono (NV70518)
Author	Yoko Saito
First Edition	Original Japanese edition published by Nihon Vogue Corp.
Copyright	©2018 Yoko Saito / NIHON VOGUE-SHA. All rights reserved.
Published by:	NIHON VOGUE Corp.
	5-6-11 Yayoicho, Nakano-Ku,
	Tokyo, Japan 164-8705

Production	Satomi Funamoto
	Terumi Ishida
	Keiko Nakajima
	Kazuko Yamada
	Orie Orimi
	Kumiko Kawano

Translation	©2021 Stitch Publications, LLC
English Translation Rights	arranged with Stitch Publications, LLC through Tuttle-Mori Agency, Inc.
Published by:	Stitch Publications, LLC, Seattle, WA, USA
	http://www.stitchpublications.com
Distributed exclusively by:	Martingale®
	18939 120th Avenue NE, Ste. 101
	Bothell, WA 98011, USA
	http://www.martingale-pub.com
Printed & Bound	KHL Printing, Singapore
ISBN	978-1-7333977-2-8
PCN	Library of Congress Control Number: 2020947778

Original Staff (Japan)	
Art & Book Design	Wakana Takemori
Styling	Terumi Inoue
Photography	Hiroaki Ishii, Noriaki Moriya (pp 48-55)
Photographic Assistance	AWABEES-UTUWA
Illustrations & Patterns	tinyeggs studio (Yumiko Oomori)
Model	Aya Inoue
Editorial Assistance	Yuko Katayama, Sakae Suzuki, Mieko Miyamoto
Editorial Staff	Tomomi Ishigami

This English edition is published by arrangement with Nihon Vogue Corp., Tokyo, in care of Tuttle-Mori Agency, Inc., Tokyo.

All rights reserved. No part of this publication may be reproduced or transmitted in any form or by any means, electronic or mechanical, including photocopy, recording, or any other information storage or retrieval systems, without written permission of the publisher. The written instructions, photographs, designs, and patterns are intended for personal, noncommercial use of the retail purchaser and protected under federal copyright laws.

The original author, publisher, and U.S.-based publisher, Stitch Publications, LLC, which has translated and compiled this material, have tried to make all of the contents as accurate as possible, and as such, no warranty is provided nor are results guaranteed. Neither the author, the original publisher, nor Stitch Publications, LLC, assumes any responsibility for any damages or losses incurred that result directly or indirectly from the information presented in this book.